Teaching Mysteries

Foundations of a Spiritual Pedagogy

Clifford Mayes

To Pam, Liz and Josh—always

Library of Congress Control Number: 2004112549

ISBN (0-7618-2950-4 paperback : alk. ppr.)

Contents

Foreword

In *Teaching Mysteries: Foundations of a Spiritual Pedagogy,* Clifford Mayes offers a biting critique of current market-driven educational reforms that celebrate a "mathetic technology," pointing to their damaging impact on the hearts, minds, and, importantly, the souls of young people and teachers. Mayes reminds readers why teaching is found by so many educators to be gripping, to be the perfect form for the fullest and richest expression of their moral passion and inner self. Such teachers have a spiritual calling to teach, and in "teaching in the spirit" seek to recreate the world and to purify and transcend themselves. To open windows on teaching of this sort, Mayes invites readers on a journey, weaving together insights drawn from poets, prophets, old and new, Buddhist, Jewish, Christian, yogis, a Yaqui shaman, sages and wise men and women whose words invite reconsideration of commitments and reevaluation of habitual ways of being with and for others. Teaching, Mayes argues, is above all else a moral and spiritual relationship, a "meeting" that seeks to awaken students to the mysteries of life and "becomes a perpetual point of departure on an eternal journey into endless ways of seeing and being." Teaching is an "exercise in intuition and a form of prayer"; to teach is to occupy sacred space and to seek to enter into holy communion with others that is simultaneously liberating, expansive, and profoundly humbling.

No soft romantic, some of Mayes' harshest criticism is directed toward those who in a celebration of the teacher's charge to nurture and to care for the young ignore that learning always and inevitably involves both death and resurrection. Learning is a form of repentance. Students, he asserts, have a right to fail, for failure and opposition are necessary to growth and to rebirth. To assist the student, the teacher, like the good parent, must be "authoritative, combining judgment (the archetypally paternal) and care (the archetypally maternal)." Love requires correction, but "the spiritual teacher [does] not let a student get caught in failure [nor does he] let him get caught in success...." Laughter proves to be one of the most powerful means the spiritual teacher has to enable the student to gain perspective, to reconsider commitments, and to overcome sin, which I take to be an inner block to growth and development. While Mayes shows that teaching is a deadly serious business, forcing those of us who enter into pedagogical relationships to confront our dark, shadowy side, teaching also reveals how hilariously funny we humans are. Heartfelt laughter makes us increasingly teachable.

Finally, Mayes calls on teachers to exercise "soul force," that sense of moral mission and commitment that flowed from Henry David Thoreau through Gandhi to Martin Luther King. *Soul force* leads to disturbing but loving acts of counter-cultural courage. Such acts are needed to protect and preserve the sacred in the face of the profane–the procrustean and armored force of the latest so-called educational reforms that menacingly march forth from Washington. It is *soul force* that lies behind *Teaching Mysteries* and behind the boldness of Mayes' own teaching and writing.

Teaching Mysteries is a powerful and provocative book that confounds the commonplaces of teaching reform, reveals the lie of detached professionalism, unflinchingly points toward the need for spiritual reclamation, and challenges and uplifts the moral imagination.

Robert V. Bullough, Jr.
The Center for the Improvement of Teacher Education and Schooling
The McKay School of Education

Acknowledgments

The premise of this book is that great teaching and deep spirituality are closely related. If that is true, then I am doubly indebted to each person whom I shall name below for shaping me both educationally and morally.

Although my mother never formally practiced her Judaism, I always felt that she lived its precepts in her unwavering honesty as a businesswoman and her passionate desire for social justice. My father's ability to access and honor emotional and intuitive truths—rare enough among men in general but especially among those whose souls had necessarily been toughened by fighting their ways through both an economic depression and a world war—showed me early in life that it was possible for a man to live according to the wisdom of the heart.

As a teenager growing up in the 1960s between the *barrios* of downtown Tucson, Arizona and the Papago Indian Reservation about 10 miles to the south, the two dearest friends of my youth, Randy Gillespie and Arnoldo Palacios, taught me by their words and actions that one's spiritual beliefs and political commitments must go hand in hand. A decade later during my graduate studies in American literature at the University of Oregon, the late Professor W. J. Handy revealed to me in his exhilarating analyses of 20th-century American fiction the deeply spiritual dimensions of much Existential philosophy and literature.

In the 1980s, while teaching at a university in Japan and also studying Zen, my spiritual journey took on more formal dimensions as I became a Christian, several years later to join the Church of Jesus Christ of Latter-day Saints. During those early days when I wrestled with what subscribing to a specific faith meant and required, not least of all in terms of my life as a scholar, two other professors at my university, Matthew Taylor and Tim McAlpine, wrestled along with me so that, together, we learned the truth of the statement that wisdom comes "even by study and also by faith" (*The Doctrine and Covenants of the Church of Jesus Christ of Latter-day Saints* 88:118). Each of us subsequently chose rather different doctrinal paths, but I like to believe that the basic love that moved and united us then continues to do so today. During that same time in my life, Father David Mayer, a priest and monk of the Society of the Divine Word, and also a professor of American literature at Nanzan University in Nagoya, Japan, helped me not only deepen my spirituality but expand it so as to reconcile it with my lifelong interest in Buddhism. A Lutheran minister, Reverend Eldon Weisheit, an earthy and tender man (whose pastoral duties unfortunately required him to forego his other calling as a stand-up comedian!), showed me that God has a sense of humor—and that a faith that cannot laugh, especially at itself, is a faith that cannot save. And I will always be indebted to the kind, wise monks of the Kanzeon Zen Center in Salt Lake City, Utah, who showed me how to deepen my meditative practice during my many hours in their *zendo*.

Now, as a teacher at Brigham Young University, I have a whole new brace of people to love and thank for their truly magnificent examples of spirituality in action. Robert V. Bullough, Jr., my former dissertation chairman at the University of Utah and now colleague at Brigham Young University, is not only the deepest thinker I have ever known but also a selfless servant to his students, community, and family. Joe Matthews, a widely respected educational leader locally and nationally, exemplifies the ability to combine educational theory and practice in the service of teachers and children. He exemplifies Joseph Smith's statement that the essence of Mormonism is faithful friendship. Even in the midst of enormous personal tragedy, Vance Randall, my departmental chair, mentor, and friend, has never failed to nurture the scholars and students in our department. Over the years, my colleague Buddy Richards has always lovingly but clearly told me when my work has fallen short of the mark. I am profoundly grateful to Brigham Young University (especially to Professor Robert Patterson, former Dean of the McKay School of Education) for granting me the resources and academic freedom to pursue a wide variety of research projects, some of them rather unconventional, but all of them, I hope, to the benefit of this great institution. My best resource at BYU has been my students, who would be the envy of any professor. Bright, loving, and dedicated, they are also amazingly patient with my many shortcomings. I have learned more from them than they from me. I am also indebted to Professor Bill Crain, of the Department of Psychology at the City College of New York and the editor of *Encounter: Education for Meaning and Social Justice*, for his wise editorial guidance during the reworking of my article "Teaching Mysteries" for publication in *Encounter*, a journal which has risen to new heights under his very able stewardship. All of these people have enabled me to accomplish whatever might be good in this book. The inevitable errors and inadequacies are entirely my own doing.

My stepdaughter, Dana, has taught me a lesson that does not come naturally to me—namely, that the spirit is fully real only when it is fully embodied. My wife, Pam, and my daughter and son, Elizabeth and Joshua, are my greatest teachers and most precious friends. Their humor, wisdom and faithfulness are the cornerstone of my life. With my wife and children, I feel I can do many things. Without them I know I could do very little, and I will never stop thanking the divine goodness that so graciously gave them to me. Indeed, in this as in all things, I acknowledge the gentle hand in my life of that God who, among all of the titles he might have taken for himself, has chosen the simple name of "Father."

Permissions

The author and publisher wish to thank the following for granting permission to quote from their works: Paramahansa Yogananda, *The Autobiography of a Yogi*. Used by permission of the Self Realization Fellowship, Los Angeles: California. Jeanne Houston, *A Mythic Life: Learning to Live Our Greater Story*. 1996. Used by permission of Harper Collins Publishers, New York: NY. Eugene Herrigel, *Zen and the Art of Archery*. 1971. Used by permission of Random House, Inc., New York: NY. Carlos Castaneda, *Journey to Ixtlan: The Lessons of Don Juan*. 1972. Used by permission of Simon and Schuster, New York: NY. Robert Bolt, *A Man for All Seasons*. 1990. Used by permission of Random House, Inc., New York: NY. Portions of *Teaching Mysteries* appeared in the author's articles "Teaching the Mysteries" (2003) in *Encounter: Education for Meaning and Social Justice,* 16(3), 43-51 and in "Personal and Archetypal Aspects of Transference and Counter-transference in the Classroom" (2002) in *Encounter: Education for Meaning and Social Justice,* 15(2), 34-49.

Introduction

The Teacher and the Rain King

I had the good fortune of studying modern American fiction in the 1970s with the great Formalist literary critic, the late W. J. Handy. One spring afternoon in 1978 on the University of Oregon campus, we were strolling back to his perennially cluttered office in Prince Lucien Campbell Hall. He had just given a memorable lecture on Saul Bellow's novel *Henderson the Rain King*. However, one question had been preoccupying me during his entire series of lectures on *Henderson*. It was a simple question but one that, in my view, went right to the heart of the greatness of this work: Why was the hero, Henderson, so funny?

Taking a long draught off of his pipe and kicking away a few dead leaves from the path we were walking on, Handy finally said, "Henderson is funny because Bellow always presents him against the backdrop of eternity." Then, as if sharing a delicious secret with me, Handy, a grin breaking over his face, almost whispered in a conspiratorial tone, "Humor is born whenever we see ourselves *sub specie aeternitatis!*"

Like humor, spirituality is born whenever one views oneself and others against the backdrops of eternity—as mortal beings who must grapple with timeless questions. These are those abiding questions that include our unique personal experiences and passionately held political convictions but always seem somehow to go just beyond them. Arising from what the Protestant theologian Paul Tillich called our "ultimate concerns," these questions involve such issues as the ambiguous ecstasies of conception and birth; the persistent uncertainties and nagging agonies of our daily existence; the riskiness of a life always lived on the edge of a mortal precipice; and—above all—the hope that, in and through all of this, we are being shaped according to a deeper purpose that folds us into itself and projects us beyond ourselves—beyond our brief individual appearance on this imperiled planet into a deathless and whole land, the land where Wallace Stevens' "palm at the end of the mind" flourishes. I believe that to lead a spiritually authentic life means wrestling with these questions in the complex and evolving conditions of a lived faith in an eternal Something or Someone.

We need to attend to spirituality much more than we presently do in our study and practice of teaching. We particularly need to attend to it in our "reflectivity" as teachers. By this term I mean introspection about why one has chosen to teach, how one teaches, and what one hopes to accomplish as a teacher. This book represents an attempt to extend teacher reflectivity into the realm of the spirit. But before explaining how I propose to do so, a few words should be said about the growth of teacher reflectivity in teacher education and teacher renewal.

As a teacher educator, I have written about a wide range of processes and techniques to deepen reflectivity, ranging from journal work and group processing to dyadic encounter and various contemplative practices (Mayes, 1998). By these means, a teacher may engage in deep introspection about herself as a teacher in order to explore why she decided to teach, the conscious and subconscious images and experiences that influence her idea of "good practice," and goals for herself and her students. The primary purpose of teacher reflectivity is to nurture and refine those images and impulses, transform them, or even expunge them in favor of more professionally and personally satisfying ones. Rooted in phenomenological and political considerations, teacher reflectivity has offered a radical alternative to the behaviorist assumptions and depersonalized, pre-packaged "skills" of competency-based teacher "training."

Often, the issues that emerge in teacher reflectivity are particularly pressing and poignant for teachers in the public schools, where corporate and political constraints and agendas do not typically honor the teacher's deeper motivations for teaching and can even do considerable institutional violence to them. By helping teachers examine the psychological and political aspects of their calling and practice, the reflectivity process has aimed at providing all teachers—in both public and non-public settings, and from kindergartens to graduate schools—with ways to define, defend, and develop themselves as educators. However, the teacher reflectivity movement has yet to adequately consider the spiritual side of the teacher's calling and practice. Although a few excellent studies have begun to explore this area (Harris, 1991; Palmer, 1998; Reinsmith, 1992; Wexler, 1996), it remains more or less *terra incognita* in teacher education and renewal (Van Manen, 1990). Biographical and political reflectivity do a great deal to help practicing and prospective teachers gain a psychosocial purchase on their work. By themselves, however, these forms of reflectivity do not go far enough for the teacher whose calling and practice has a spiritual dimension.

Of course, one's spirituality can be either formal and systematic, involving commitment to a certain faith, informal and strictly personal, or a combination of both. In any case, the person who grapples with issues like these and makes them the foundation of her life has, in my view, crossed the threshold into the spiritual domain. If that person is a teacher, then her spirituality will affect her professional identity and practice. To think spiritually about oneself as a teacher is to engage in what I have called "spiritual reflectivity" (Mayes, 2001). It is to see one's teaching against an eternal backdrop. Not all teachers feel a need to see themselves and their craft spiritually. People become teachers for many good reasons that are not necessarily (or not consciously) grounded in ontological soil. But for those teachers to whom spiritual issues are important, this book may help them hone their spiritual reflectivity and practice by studying some great teacher-exemplars from various spiritual traditions.

Some of the spiritual teaching-masters whom we will visit in this book are found in literature, as in Robert Bolt's portrayal of the 16th-century statesman (and later Roman Catholic saint) Thomas More in Bolt's play *A Man for All Seasons*; some appear in biographies—such as the account of the life of Paramahansa Yogananda, the great 20th-century Hindu saint, in *Autobiography of a Yogi*; or Black Elk, the 19th-century Ogalala Sioux medicine man, in *Black Elk Speaks*; some reside in an intriguing region that moves on the misty boundaries between biography and fiction, such as Don Juan, the modern Yaqui medicine man, in Carlos Castaneda's *Journey to Ixtlan*. And some walk the halls of academia, such as the Jewish theologian Martin Buber, author of the 20th-century theological classic *I and Thou* and also a seminal essay entitled "On Teaching." My hope is that in encountering these exemplars

One

The Politics of the Spirit
in the Classroom

Teaching in the spirit can never be merely a "professional" act that bears little or no relationship to one's "personal" life. It cannot be the function of a fragment of a divided self. If it is, then it ceases to be an expression of the true self and becomes (as Marx insisted) a form of alienation from it. Such teachers, estranged from themselves because estranged from their work, have little to offer the student spiritually. In many cases, this is due to the fact that teachers are often under relentless pressure to become pedagogical agents of a corporate state which would rob them and their students of their unique ethical and spiritual identities. From at least the beginning of the 20th century, the American teacher has constantly had to fight against state and federal reforms which, based on the utilitarian philosophy of social efficiency, have attempted to turn schools into training grounds for "worker-citizens"— differentiated cogs in the great social machine (Spring, 1976; see also Cremin, 1988; Kliebard, 1986; Ravitch, 2000; Spring, 2000; Tyack, 1974). This movement to transform teachers, administrators, and schools into servants of the "cult of efficiency" (Callahan, 1962) will probably continue to grow and exert increasing dominion over American education throughout the 21st century as transnational corporate capitalism continues to create and corner ever larger markets (Bell, 1976; Giddens, 1990; Lasch, 1995).

Forced into ever tighter managerial roles and technocratic functions, the American public school teacher is counseled, cajoled and (when that fails) forced to deliver a curriculum devised by "experts" in pursuit of higher standardized test scores that are designed to monitor the student's acquisition of marketable skills. In such things as "School-to-Career" programs, the focus is almost exclusively on marketability. The Reagan administration's agenda for reform as outlined in the two reports *A Nation at Risk* and *Excellence in Education,* the Clinton administration's *Goals 2000: Educate America,* and, perhaps most perniciously of all, the Bush administration's *No Child Left Behind Act,* compel schools to emphasize the technical skills and knowledge that will adapt students to the bottom-line realities of the "new global economy." Schools that fail to conform to this philosophically hollow and pedagogically disastrous program (which not only abandons the larger purposes of education in a democracy but is probably not even an effective way to achieve its own monetary goals) can expect public censure, denial of federal funds, and even closure. Teachers at these schools face pay reduction, denial of tenure, and even dismissal. As has always been true with norm-referenced testing, children who cannot or will not fit into the "norm" for whatever psychological, socio-economic, cultural, or spiritual reasons, will not do well (Jones, Jones, & Hargrove, 2003). As has been clear in educational research for at least the last four decades, such tests do not measure "ability" and "intelligence" in all of their incalculable richness but are largely just indicators of the "cultural capital" that the student brings to the testing table (Bourdieu, 1976). Nothing predicts a student's score on the SAT as accurately as his parents' socioeconomic status (Riordan, 1997).

The unmistakable message in such "reforms" is that schools are to become servants and suppliers to what Giddens (1990) has identified as the four major loci of power in the postmodern world: the world military order, the nation-state system, the transnational capitalist economy, and the new international division of labor that "out-sources" menial piecework at the lowest possible wages to third-world employees and pays the highest rewards to the "symbolic analysts" of the most privileged nations.

The spiritual teacher's calling, therefore, inevitably has a political aspect, for in terms of both *what* is taught and *how* it is taught, the spiritual call to teach inherently represents an ethical challenge to the political and psychological forces of inauthenticity and oppression that would change the classroom from a haven for existential encounter into a training ground for corporate functionaries. Besides, spiritual practices that ignore political injustice may easily become self absorbed piety, which is not really spiritual at all because it has failed to respond to the cry of human suffering. Spiritual teaching must therefore promote not only personal but also social liberation from "unrighteous dominion"—that is, the attempt "to exercise control or dominion or compulsion upon the souls of the children of men, in any degree of unrighteousness..." (*The Doctrine and Covenants of the Church of Jesus Christ of Latter-day Saints* 121: 37).

From a Roman Catholic perspective, Harris (1991) has also discussed the socially transformative potential—indeed, the social duty—of teaching in the spirit:

> If I am to be a complete human being, no other vocation is worthy of me. Thus I answer the question "For what?" or "What is this grace of power toward?" quite simply. The grace of power is directed toward the re-creation of the world. Teaching, when seen as an act of the religious imagination, is an act of incarnating subject matter in ways which (or in order to) reveal subject matter so that subjects, in communication with each other, are able to exercise power: the capacity and ability to act receptively, intelligently, humanly, responsibly, and religiously in transforming the universe. (p. 113)

Shelley said that the poet is "the unacknowledged legislator of the world." I would say that the ethically committed teacher is—and that the poet is one type of such a teacher. Such teachers affirm God in all of our wastelands—psychological, political and spiritual. They proclaim the Light in the darkness. They announce the unequivocal *Word* over the chattering banality of slick commercialism. They are what Bullough, Patterson and I have called the "teacher-prophet" (Bullough, Patterson, & Mayes, 2002). Each teacher-prophet sees this light and hears this Word in different ways depending upon his personal convictions and academic curriculum. Yet each is a witness to the divine reality that called him to his prophetic work and continues to sustain him in it.

We see an example of a politically prophetic teacher who is grounded in his spiritual convictions in Robert Bolt's play *A Man for All Seasons*, which deals with the eventual martyrdom of Sir Thomas More, who was later canonized by the Roman Catholic Church as St.

Thomas More. More, the gifted writer of *Utopia* and other influential works of the late 15th early 16th century, was one of the finest intellectual and spiritual flowers of Renaissance humanism. As a statesman of incomparable gifts, he became the Lord Chancellor of England in 1529 by the appointment of King Henry VIII, who counted More as one of his closest friends and advisors. More, however, resigned his position in 1531 when Henry broke from Rome to establish the Church of England, putatively for theological reasons but actually in order to gain a divorce from his wife, Catherine of Aragon, which the Pope would not grant. Parliament also passed a bill in 1534 that required all subjects of the King to take an oath in which they would swear fealty to the King above all other foreign sovereigns, including the Pope. As a profoundly committed Catholic, More, an intensely patriotic Englishman, could not see his way clear to support Henry's break with Rome and take the oath; yet, ever the astute lawyer, he also hoped that by remaining silent on these issues he would preserve his family and himself on the strength of the legal precept that "qui tacet consentire"—in silence is consent. Neither More's good faith, genuine devotion to King and country, or lawyerly maneuvers, however, could save him, and he was arrested, placed in the Tower, and finally beheaded in 1535.

Throughout the play Sir Thomas teaches his family and friends by both word and example that if, despite our best efforts, we cannot avoid a conflict between the law of man and the law of God, then the law of God must take precedence, no matter the price to oneself or even the state. Indeed, when More is enjoined by no less a personage than Cardinal Wolsey to "do his duty" as a leader of the nation and compromise his conscience in order to preserve social order, More observes that there is ultimately nothing *more* destabilizing to a state than "when statesmen forsake their own private conscience for the sake of their public duties," for when they do so, "they lead their country by a short route to chaos" (Bolt, 1990, p. 22). Thomas' life and death in Bolt's play bear witness to the idea that no political cause, however compelling, can prosper if it is not built on the rock of spiritual vision. Any political program that does not finally rest upon such a base runs the risk of becoming spiritually disoriented and of then resorting to unrighteous dominion to establish and maintain itself.

Everywhere, in every circumstance, Thomas, the loyal Englishman but even more loyal son of the Church, teaches his friends and family—explicitly when possible, implicitly when it is too unsafe to speak directly—that their duty to the transcendent truth of God supersedes the demands of the temporal state. His every action in the play—and especially his martyrdom—conveys the lesson that temporal power and purposes must always be contained in a higher vision. If they are not, they worsen the very evils that they propose to cure. Indeed, so committed is Thomas to his role as a teacher that he makes it very clear early on in the play that there is no higher role that a person can fill. In a touching dialogue near the beginning of the play, a young scholar who has just graduated from Oxford, Richard Rich, asks Thomas More for employment. More offers Rich the position of a teacher. However, Rich—who at the end of the play bears false testimony against More in order to gain political advancement—is an ambitious young man who harbors grander social pretensions and political ambitions than being a teacher could satisfy. He flatly refuses More's offer. More persists:

> More: Why not be a teacher? You'd be a fine teacher.
> Perhaps even a great one.
>
> Rich: And if I was, who would know it?
>
> More: You. Your pupils. Your friends. God. Not a bad
> public, that! (Bolt, 1990, pp. 8-9)

Still Rich refuses, missing Sir Thomas' point that the spiritually called teacher possesses a power and satisfaction that outshine and outlast any program or preferment that is merely political. Sustained by his higher ethical vision, the prophet-teacher resists—and exhorts his students to resist—the forces of both spiritual and political darkness. He finds the wherewithal to do this not because of public acclaim or great remuneration—which are only very rarely the teacher's lot—but by remaining true to his original calling. The spiritually called teacher understands his calling and practices his art in the light of his spiritual commitment; they buttress his life as a teacher, no matter what his subject-matter. For as Thomas declares at his trial—attempting even then to educate the very men who will presently condemn him to death—"In matters of conscience, the loyal subject is more bounden to be loyal to his conscience than to any other thing…" (Bolt, 1990, p. 153). This has always been the ethical and political message of spiritually committed teachers as they struggle "against principalities, against powers, against the rulers of the darkness of this world, against spiritual wickedness in high places" (Ephesians 6: 12).

Although the setting is different for the spiritual teacher in the postmodern state than it was for More in the renaissance one, his challenge is still the same—to expose and denounce the idols of the corporate state, which now worships electronic and economic gods. Such a teacher refuses to bow the knee to these gods whether they are clothed in the trappings of conservative or liberal rhetoric. For in both cases, the teacher-prophet recognizes the extraordinary peril that curricula built on the corporate approach to education represent to the minds and souls of students and teachers.

Is there any hope for a world in which so many individuals "have so lost themselves to the collective Moloch [that they] cannot be rescued from it by any reference, however eloquent, to the absolute whose kingdom Moloch has usurped?" (Buber, 1985, p. 110). Regarding this question, a great teacher-prophet of the 20th century, the Jewish theologian Martin Buber, has asserted:

> Nothing remains but what rises above the abyss of today's monstrous problems, as above every abyss of every time: the wing-beat of the spirit and the creative word. But he who can see and hear out of unity will also behold and discern again what can be beheld and discerned eternally. *The educator who helps to bring man back to his own unity will help to put him again face to face with God.* (Buber, 1985, p. 117. Emphasis added.)

I am not suggesting, of course, that schools must not include practical issues and programs that may serve the student in his future occupation in the corporate state in which that student must, after all, exist—and which he may even help to transform and humanize. Clearly, these more pragmatic goals are an important function of schooling—and one that parents justifiably expect their schools to perform (Purpel & Shapiro, 1995). However, when we have reached a pass where (to rephrase President Coolidge) "the business of American schools is business," then we have gone too far down the road of the social-efficiency curriculum, a path that public schooling entered in the first two decades of the 20th century under Snedden and Possner and to which it has now been forced to commit itself at the expense of virtually everything else. Thus it is that we now find ourselves in real danger of losing the prophetic functions of education by worshipping the Golden Calf of the idolatrous Bottom Line (Cremin, 1988; Kliebard, 1986).

During an education symposium at the American Buddhist university Naropa, His Holiness the Dalai Lama observed:

> From my rough impression of the Western educational system, although it is very impressive to see the high standard of the intellectual facilities and also many other resources, one thing that is becoming quite apparent is that the dimension of enhancing and developing the heart is lacking." (1997, p. 6)

In my experience teaching educators and educational leaders, I have often heard them bemoan the fact that American education is becoming ever more "heartless." Parker Palmer is quite correct in his diagnosis that "education is dull because we have driven the sacred out of it" (1998, p. 10).

Now, for teachers whose calling is interwoven with their spirituality, banishing the sacred obviously creates a terrible tension—one that often chokes off the deeper forces that inspired them to become teachers in the first place. I maintain that a good deal of teacher burnout is the result of teachers' concluding that they cannot remain true to their individual sense of spiritual calling in an increasingly technocratic school system. As Lortie (1975) noted almost three decades ago, most teachers are motivated by such "psychic rewards" as a passion for their subject, a sense of social purpose, delight and personal growth in increased emotional intimacy with their students, and deep moral fulfillment in seeing students blossom intellectually, emotionally, and spiritually under their care. The Jungian psychologist Irene de Castillejo's observations about general practitioners would seem to apply as well to teachers. General practitioners, she says,

> have been vociferous about their unjust remuneration and inferior status in the medical hierarchy, but I have never heard them mention what is much more likely to be the fundamental nature of their unhappiness: that the *archetype of a healer* which has sustained and nourished them throughout the centuries has fallen from their shoulders leaving them as little cogs in the great machine of modern medical practice. It is not a greater share of the world's wealth they lack, but "mana." (1973, p. 22)

I do not have any magic formulas for reforming the conflicted system of American public education from the outside so that the teacher does not have to constantly negotiate these political and institutional demands. In fact, as both a student and teacher of the history of American education, I do not believe such formulas exist. There is simply the daily struggle for the teacher to teach as passionately and compassionately as he can—against formidable odds. What I do have, however, and what I offer here, is my best attempt to present the perspectives and practices of a few masters of spiritual teaching. I believe that studying the lives of these masters is important because we as teachers need to be able to reflect and draw upon spiritual images and exemplars of teaching in order to recall, refresh, and magnify that sense of vocation which is our essential moral food. My hope is that educators and educational leaders may come to know these remarkable people better—as I have in the course of writing this book—and that they can use these masters' examples to touch the wellsprings of their own calling and thereby replenish their own practice. Thus, amid the institutional dilemmas that beset us all as teachers, we may yet find ways to review and renew ourselves pedagogically, socially and spiritually.

Topics for Discussion

Do you agree that spiritual teaching inevitably has a political dimension as is claimed in this chapter? There are those who would argue that when spirituality becomes too involved in politics, it loses its transcendent perspective on people and events because it gets too embroiled in the passionate but passing issues of the day. Where do you stand on this topic?

Are your political commitments and spiritual commitments interrelated? If so, in what ways and to what extent? Do they relate to your reasons for being a teacher? Do they consciously or unconsciously affect the way you teach—or plan to teach?

Topics for Research

Liberation Theologians argue that the Kingdom of God can be established on the earth only through the spiritually inspired political activism of the faithful on behalf of and in identification with the poor in all countries and cultures. Trace the rise of Liberation Theology in the second half of the 20th century and how it has expressed itself in vari-

Topics for Research (continued)

ous liberatory pedagogies such as those of Ivan Illich and Paolo Freire. Also if studying liberatory pedagogies in the course of researching this paper has had an effect on how you teach or plan to teach, discuss this as well.

Look at the life and writings of such 19th-century female educational reformers such as Mother Mary Seton and Catherine Beecher to examine the effects of their religious commitments on their political vision of education.

Critically evaluate Philip Wexler's (1996) book, *Holy Sparks: Social Theory, Education and Religion*, in which he uses his commitment to mystical Judaism as a foundation for his own version of liberatory pedagogy. Also, discuss the effects, if any, that this study may have on your own classroom practice.

knew thee," says Jehovah to Jeremiah, one of Israel's greatest teachers, "and before thou camest forth out of the womb, I sanctified thee, and I ordained thee a prophet unto the nations" (Jeremiah 1:5).

As important as the issuance of God's call, is the recipient's response. Without that, the divine summons is issued in vain. For, others will remain untouched if they do not hear the necessary voice of the teacher-prophetess. Once a teacher has felt and been fertilized by the spirit, she must be true to this calling. She must bring the "pregnancy" to term by "bearing" witness to the divine hope that has invested her with its intelligence and love. Otherwise, Jonah-like, she will spend her days attempting to deny the Voice and mute the message. If she does assume her mantle as a teacher-prophetess, bearing testimony in the form of her teaching, then she will grow both spiritually and pedagogically. What and how she teaches will increasingly reflect her ontological vision. How this happens from teacher to teacher will naturally vary given differences in curricula, institutional contexts, and the needs and abilities of her students. Yet in each case, teaching becomes the teacher's personal echo of the voice of God in the classroom—no matter how large or small, how conventional or unconventional that classroom.

It is important to stress that none of this requires any specific proclamations in the classroom about the teacher's personal faith or doctrinal commitments, which, in almost all cases, are wisely prohibited in the public school classroom. And why would the teacher make the classroom a pulpit for explicit statements of her faith anyway? Explicit declarations of belief rarely impress and almost never convince. Rather, it is the lived example of the teacher—in the class, with the class, and for the class—that conveys the message. This leaves the student free to appropriate the message in the ways that make the most sense to her.

In the spiritual classic *Autobiography of a Yogi* we see many examples of teaching about divinity through the teacher's character, not his preaching. In this manner, the great 20th-century Hindu saint Paramahansa Yogananda was first granted a vision of God in the face of his teacher, Sri Yukteswar. But this happened not so much in what the guru said to his young *chela* but through who the guru *was*—a teacher-prophet who had spent a lifetime becoming refined in the crucible of his calling. "Gratefully I accept your authority in every detail of my life," Yogananda promised upon first meeting his guru by a miraculous series of events. But he added the slightly impudent caveat, "on one condition." Probably anticipating the question of his young student be-

fore it was asked, Sri Yukteswar politely but coyly responded, "Yes?"
"That you promise to reveal God to me!"

> An hour-long verbal tussle ensued. A master's word cannot
> be falsified; it is not lightly given. The implications in the
> pledge open out vast metaphysical vistas. A guru must be
> on intimate terms with the Creator before he can obligate
> Him to appear! I sensed Sri Yukteswar's divine unity, and
> was determined, as his disciple, to press my advantage.
> "You are of exacting disposition." Then Master's consent
> rang out with compassionate finality: "Let your wish be my
> wish." A life-long shadow lifted from my heart; the vague
> search, hither and yon, was over. I had found eternal shelter
> in a true guru. (1946, p. 122)

Of course, few of us can manifest divinity to our students in nearly
as dramatic or complete a fashion as Sri Yuketswar did. But for a
teacher whose practice rests on spiritual foundations, she must try, and
never stop trying, to answer her students' implicit cry for a vision of the
divine by answering in the best faith possible, "Let your wish be my
wish!" Whether she is teaching art or astronomy, advanced placement
or special education, she must be as true as possible to this call, matur-
ing under its influence. And finally she must communicate it to her students in ways that will empower them to come closer to the spirit as
each of them uniquely sees and understands it.

The challenge to spiritually visionary teachers in the inhospitable
circumstances of modern American education is not merely to maintain
their vision but to extend it by using those very social and institutional
forces that oppose it as a refining fire. In this way, they may strengthen
their commitments and discover an ever clearer prophetic voice. Like
all moral growth, this is accomplished through prayer, reflection, and
action. Increasingly purified, the teacher's voice, oscillating more and
more closely to the rhythms of the divine, echoes (through the many
voices of her changed students) beyond the classroom, beyond the
school, and into the hearts and consciences of the people. Thus the
teacher-prophetess responds to the Lord's command to Jeremiah to be a
"voice to the nation."

Speaking of the prophetic calling of the teacher, the Jewish theologian Martin Buber has called him "the great representative of the one
true God":

The revelation does not pour itself into the world through him who receives it as through a funnel; it comes to him and seizes his whole elemental being in all its particular nature and fuses with it. The man, too, who is the "mouth" of the revelation, is indeed this, not a speaking-tube or any kind of instrument, but an organ, which sounds according to its own laws; and to sound means to *modify*. (1958, p. 117)

This is why the approaches to teacher education that see good practice as merely the mastery of depersonalized, decontextualized "competencies" that can be sequentially listed and systematically implanted in the "preservice teacher" are fundamentally immoral. They run roughshod over the ontological ground of the teacher's vocation. By neglecting the prospective teacher's political, ethical and spiritual impulses and interests, such forms of teacher "training" attempt to reduce her to an uncritical pedagogical tool of a web of national and transnational corporate interests and organizations who wish for nothing more than that schools might produce only obedient "worker-citizens" for the new "global economy" (Spring, 2000). Instead of promoting personal and political liberation, teaching is now forced into becoming an agent of psycho-social domination of both the teacher and student (Freire, 1970). Competency-based teacher training is a parody of teacher education.

What we need instead—and what in my experience many teachers want—is socially and spiritually "redemptive teaching" (Wexler, 1986, p. 141). An essential element of teacher education and teacher renewal must be to help prospective and practicing teachers define and develop this vision, which will naturally vary from teacher to teacher. As William James said, we live in "a pluralistic universe" of many truths and many types of divine callings. If this were not so, then teacher-prophetesses would all sound the same and convey the same message.

Meeting as Destiny

Because the call to teach is a matter of destiny, it is not surprising that the meeting of the teacher and student sometimes has an aura of inevitability about it. Indeed, the literature on sacred teaching clearly attests that the meeting of the spiritual teacher and her student is no accident if their learning relationship is destined to be a spiritual one. As Buber said, "all real living is meeting" (1958, p. 11). When the teacher and student meet as a matter of destiny, the classroom becomes a place of "real living," a counter-cultural space of life as opposed to the surrounding culture of death—that morass of crass and fast sex with neither love nor responsibility; a culture of the ludicrous moral prostration of the individual before digital and automotive gods; one that promotes the over-consumption of drugs, drink and food that surfeit our senses but can never completely quiet the cry of the heart that has betrayed itself. Yet, that heart can be revived in the "real meeting" between teacher and student in the existentially authentic zone of the classroom. Whether it is a bit of ground under a shade-tree in the desert or an inner-city classroom, this teacher and student occupy an alternative space—a space "where obedience to truth is practiced" (Palmer, 1983, p. 69). In this classroom students can discover their own callings because the teacher, true to her calling, is teaching spiritually. The miracle of spiritual teaching consists, then, in the fact that the teacher transmits spiritual energy to her students through the enabling medium of the curriculum. Thus, whether the subject is Trotsky or transistors, ballet or Blake, any curricular ground is potentially holy ground.

Yognanda's first encounter with Sri Yuketswar exemplifies the meeting of teacher and student as destiny. Wandering through the streets of Banaras, India one ordinary afternoon, "I turned my head," recalled Yogananda,

> to survey a narrow, inconspicuous lane. A Christ-like man in the ochre robes of a swami stood motionless at the end of the lane. Instantly and anciently familiar he seemed to me.... Retracing my steps as though wing-shod, I reached the narrow lane. My quick glance revealed the quiet figure, steadily gazing in my direction. A few eager steps and I was at his feet. "Gurudeva!" The divine face was the one I had seen in a thousand visions. These halcyon eyes, in a leonine head with pointed beard and flowing locks, had oft peered through the gloom of my nocturnal reveries, holding a promise I had not yet fully understood. "O my own, you have come to me!" My guru uttered the words again and again in Bengali, his voice tremulous with joy. "How many years I have waited for you!" (1946, pp. 106-107)

When the poet John Neihardt met the great Ogalala medicine man Black Elk, it was also an instance of a destiny-laden encounter. Neihardt, who was writing an epic poem cycle entitled *Song of the Messiah,* wanted to interview Black Elk about the Messiah Movement that had accompanied the tragic defeat of the Lakota nation in the late

1800s. On the way, Niehardt's Indian guide says that it is hardly likely that Black Elk will have anything to say to him on this subject, much less to his white companion, having kept an almost complete silence regarding it these many years. But this was a meeting that had been ordained and arranged in eternity:

> It was a dead-end road that led through the treeless yellow hills to Black Elk's home—a one-room log cabin with weeds growing out of the dirt roof.... When we arrived, Black Elk was standing outside a shade made of pine boughs. It was noon. When we left, after sunset, Flying Hawk said, "That was kind of funny, the way the old man seemed to know you were coming!" My son remarked that he had the same impression.... [Later, they all sat on the ground and began to smoke.] Black Elk, with his near-blind stare fixed on the ground, seemed to have forgotten us. I was about to break the silence by way of getting something started, when the old man looked up to Flying Hawk, the interpreter, and said (in Sioux, for he knew no English): "As I sit here, I can feel in this man beside me a strong desire to know the things of the Other World. He has been sent to learn what I know, and I will teach him.... There is so much to teach you. What I know was given to me for men and it is true and it is beautiful. Soon I shall be under the grass and it will be lost. You were sent to save it, and you must come back so that I can teach you. (Black Elk, xvi-xvii)

A sense of prophetic destiny also surrounded the meeting in 1961 of Carlos Castaneda, a young graduate student in anthropology, with the Yaqui shaman Don Juan. At first, the callow Castaneda thinks that he can pump Don Juan for useful field data about the properties of certain plants in the Sonora desert. But this meeting is not, as Castaneda imagined, just another ethnographic interview. Indeed, the iconoclastic Don Juan immediately plucks Castaneda out of his superficial, social-scientific world-view, magically flinging him headlong into a dizzying series of shifting universes and transformative mysteries until Castaneda himself has become a shaman. About half-way through this process, Don Juan reminisces (somewhat mercilessly as he tends to do) about how he and his comically unwitting apprentice met.

> "The decision about who can be a warrior and who can only be a hunter is not up to us. That decision is in the realm of the powers that guide men.... Those forces guided

you to me; they took you to that bus depot, remember? Some clown brought you to me. A perfect omen, a clown pointing you out.... And then the other perfect omen [of a dog named after an important plant to Yaqui medicine men] playing with you. See what I mean?" His weird logic was overwhelming. His words created visions of myself succumbing to something awesome and unknown, something which I had not bargained for, and which I had not conceived existed.... (1972, p. 119)

The spiritually called teacher strives to cultivate her sense of when a student wanders into her classroom as simply a random event—or when, on the other hand, destiny has scheduled the encounter. Not every encounter between teacher and student is prophetic, but those that are announce themselves to the sensitized teacher in many ways, some of them improbable. For instance, Buber asks the reader to imagine a young teacher entering a classroom full of boys at the beginning of the term—a most unlikely site for the emergence of the delicate operations of the Spirit! The students are noisy, some are rude, a few even seem to be poised on the edge of their seats to catch the teacher in the smallest mistake and thus sabotage any attempt on his part to establish authority. Understandably defensive, the teacher is at once inclined to bark out orders,

to say No, to say No to everything rising against him from beneath.... And if one starts from beneath one perhaps never arrives above, but everything comes down. But then his eyes meet a face which strikes him. It is not a beautiful face nor particularly intelligent; but it is a real face, or rather, the chaos preceding the cosmos of a real face. On it he reads a question which is something different from the general curiosity.... And he, the young teacher, addresses this face. He says nothing very ponderous or important, he puts an ordinary introductory question: "What did you talk about last in geography? The Dead Sea? Well, what about the Dead Sea?" But there was obviously something not quite usual in the question, for the answer he gets is not the ordinary schoolboy answer; the boy begins to *tell a story*. Some months earlier he had stayed for a few hours on the shores of the Dead Sea and it is of this he tells. He adds: "And everything looked to me as if it had been created a day before the rest of creation." Quite unmistakably he had only in this moment made up his mind to talk about it. In the meantime his face has changed. It is no longer quite as chaotic as before. And the class has fallen silent. They all listen. The class, too, is no longer a chaos. Something has happened. The young teacher has started from above. (1985, pp. 112-3)

This "starting" and meeting "from above" in the classroom may happen only with the teacher's help. I imagine that God must find it very difficult to build upon the encounter between a teacher and student if the teacher is not prepared for the encounter—if, that is, she has not previously exercised her moral freedom such that now, at this critical juncture with her student, she has the kind of prophetic soul that can intuit and convey a sense of the divine *to* that student. All of the voices from the various prophetic traditions have told us that we are co-creators of history with God. This is also true in the classroom. We participate with God in working out our personal spiritual history as teachers. We also join with him in our students' moral development. And through these means (if we have continually worked to purify ourselves) we are his instruments; we contribute to his world-historical purpose of creating a new earth.

In the prophetic meeting of teacher and student exists the embryo of their future educational relationship. All real living is meeting. And all spiritual teaching may grow out of that meeting if the teacher has heeded the call to be a teacher-prophetess. Then, like Isaiah, she can respond to the Creator's question "Whom shall I send, and who will go for us?" with the words "Here am I; send me" (Isaiah 6: 8).

When Brigham Young first met Joseph Smith—the first president of my church—it was clearly a case of meeting as destiny and teaching as revelation. Said Brigham recalling his first sessions with the young prophet-teacher:

> I never saw anyone, until I met Joseph Smith, who could tell me anything about the character, personality, and dwelling place of God, or anything satisfactory about angels, or the relationship of man to his Maker. Yet I was as diligent as any man need be to try and find out these things.... When I saw Joseph Smith, he took heaven, figuratively speaking, and brought it down to earth; and he took the earth, brought it up and opened up, in plainness and simplicity, the things of God.... What a delight it was to hear Brother Joseph talk upon the great principles of eternity; he would bring them down to the capacity of a child,

and he would unite heaven with earth. (*Journal of Discourses* 4: 54, 5: 332, 16: 46)

The destined meeting of the student with an inspired teacher results in an education of radical simplicity—a "plainness" that "unites heaven with earth." In what and how she teaches, she unites the temporal and the eternal. How could a student ever forget such a teacher? She has ushered the student through the halls of the curriculum into the chambers of the sacred.

Topics for Discussion

Do you find the idea of the teacher-prophetess personally empowering to you as a teacher, or do you find that it places a greater burden on you than you wish to assume as a teacher? Do you find it empowering in some ways and perhaps overpowering in others?

As a student, have you ever met a teacher as a matter of destiny? How has your life since that time confirmed your initial impression that your meeting was fated?

Conversely, as a teacher, have you ever met a student as a matter of destiny? And again, how has your life since that time confirmed your initial impression that your meeting was fated?

Do you agree with the author that *any* subject can offer the teacher a chance to communicate the divine to her students? And even if you agree with the author, do you agree with him that *all* subjects are equally able to fulfill this function?

Topics for Research

Looking through a spiritual text that is or has been important to you, do you find images and instances of prophets fulfilling the role of teacher? Do you find other kinds of teachers in that text who are not

Topics for Research (continued)

"prophetic" but inadequate and possibly even dangerous? What seem to be the qualities of a teacher, according to your spiritual text, which make her "prophetic"?

Examine the "teacher reflectivity" movement in the United States that has arisen over approximately the last two decades. Trace its rise and discuss to what degree, if at all, it has been successful in challenging the "competency-based" approaches to teacher education.

Three

Lucre and Wonder

Tension and Growth in Teaching

If the teacher-prophet stays true to his calling in his thought, heart and practice, he gains a deepening understanding of the educator's power to transform himself, his students, and his world. But how can the teacher remain faithful to this rigorous vocation—especially in a society that has often used educators as scapegoats for many of its social and ethical ills over the last century? (Parkerson & Parkerson, 2001; Watras, 1996). I believe that for the teacher an answer lies in the notion of the individual's eternal evolution—an idea that is central not only in my faith community but in certain others as well (de Chardin, 1975). It is not enough for the teacher merely to maintain his vision. A static vision is soon a dead one. What is necessary in order for him to grow in his critique of and resistance to the dominant socioeconomic order is constant spiritual growth.

Paradoxically, the very criticism that threatens the teacher in the anti-intellectual environment of American culture can also spur him on in his evolutionary process (Hofstadter, 1963). The teacher may even view this political and cultural opposition as part of a larger cosmic dynamic; for, "without opposition there is no progression," as Blake wrote. A scripture from my religious tradition also makes this point quite forcefully: "For it must needs be that there is an opposition in all things. If not so[,] righteousness could not be brought to pass, neither wickedness, neither holiness nor misery, neither good nor bad. Wherefore all things must be a compound in one... (*Book of Mormon,* 2 Nephi 2: 11).

Instead of buckling under the weight of the public misunderstandings that often attend one's decision to teach ("But you're so bright! Why in the world would you want to become a teacher?"), the spiritually called teacher may understand them as grist for the mill. For it is simply a fact that others will often misunderstand the teacher's sense of calling. Some people will even make light of it, especially those who see teaching as merely keeping children in line, pounding cultural platitudes into them, or priming them to make money.

> We must acknowledge that some people, some parents, some teachers may not heed or attend to the call of pedagogy. We may even acknowledge ourselves of having been deaf to the calling of parenting or teaching. And if we haven't heard its calling, how then can we comprehend its nature? For those who cannot hear, reflecting on pedagogy as a calling is just sentimental nonsense, or at best a useless exercise. (Van Manen, 1982, p. 297)

This should not cause us to despair, however. In reflectively sharpening his sense of calling on the whetstone of criticism, the teacher learns important social and ethical lessons that clarify his prophetic voice. This is a necessary process, for it has always been the function of the prophet to clear a place in the national wilderness, to make the road straight for the appearance of a message which the nation would otherwise be unprepared to receive.

> Then said they unto [John the Baptist], Who art thou? that we may give an answer to them that sent us. What sayest thou of thyself. He said, I am the voice of one crying in the wilderness, Make straight the way of the Lord, as said the prophet Esaias. (John 1: 19-23)

The Calling and the Crucible

It is a serious responsibility to take on the mantle of the teacher. Aware of his weaknesses, the spiritually motivated teacher continually attempts to develop not only his understanding of his subject matter but also his moral nature, for the physician must first heal himself. In my faith, this responsibility to evolve never ends but is a matter of what we call "eternal progression." This process also involves the teacher as a cultural pioneer—but only if, as Yogananda taught, he is "on intimate terms with the Creator..." (1996, p. 123). Through his teaching, the spiritually called teacher purifies himself in his reflectivity and practice so that he may more clearly receive and communicate the Spirit. In this refining process, money cannot be a primary factor. Although not necessarily indifferent to money, this kind of teacher has always seen it as at best a distant second to his higher purposes. Even a cursory look at the history of teaching in the United States shows that this is so (Parkerson & Parkerson, 2001).

In the 19th century many American teachers' sense of mission "possessed quasi-spiritual properties" in their desire to inculcate moral and civic virtues (Mattingly, 1975, p. 63). Especially in antebellum America, many teachers saw themselves in "ministerial" terms that stemmed from "the evangelical origins of teaching" in the U.S. (Mattingly, 1975, p. 63). Not a few teachers of this period were inspired by Gladden's socially proactive theology of "The Social Gospel" (Cremin, 1988). Their work ranged from teaching the newly arrived immigrants in Jane Addams's Settlement Houses to the recently "liberated" slaves in the South (Cremin, 1988; Jones, 1980). Clearly, the socially transformative power of public education and the social implications of the Gospel were tightly intertwined in Gladden's scenario, in which teachers would instill in children those virtues that would lead to "a Christianizing of the social order... [and the establishment] of the Kingdom of God on earth" (Cremin, 1988, p. 22).

The towering American female educators of the mid- to late-19th century such as Mother Mary Seton and Catherine Beecher saw teaching as primarily a religious "vocation" (Sklar, 1973). Catherine Beecher even proclaimed that it was the teacher who would raise the ethical and intellectual level of the nation's youth so as to prepare the nation for the return of Christ and the establishment of his millennial kingdom in the United States (Sklar, 1973). Tyack (1989) thus concluded that "throughout most of the 19th-century..., for many teachers a powerful Protestant-republican ideology of service gave resonance to [their] work" (p. 417). Perhaps we are hearing contemporary echoes of this historical motif in Lortie's discovery that "psychic rewards" matter more to teachers than "external rewards." At any rate, Lortie's dichotomy mirrors Buber's statement that a teacher with a sense of spiritual calling does not "treat money, embodied non-being, 'as if it were God'" (1958, p. 106).

The theme of dedication to a higher impulse than that of accumulating money and fame abounds in accounts of the lives of the greatest spiritual teachers—and nowhere with such vigor and humor as in the Yaqui shaman Don Juan. Early in their relationship, Carlos Castaneda offered to pay the teacher for his "services." "My explanation," said Castaneda, "was that I wanted bona fide information about the use of plants, thus I had asked him to be my informant. I had even offered to pay him for his time and trouble."

> "You should take the money," I said. "This way we both would feel better. I then could ask you anything I want to because you would be working for me and I would pay you for it. What do you think of that?" He looked at me contemptuously and made an obscene sound with his mouth, making his lower lip vibrate by exhaling with great force. "That's what I think of it!" he said and laughed hysterically at the look of utmost surprise I must have had on my face. (1972, p. 47)

In a more decorous vein, Paramahansa Yogananda recalled the great Indian teacher Bhaduri Mahasaya, who was also known as "the levitating saint" because, like St. Teresa of Avila, he would often rise off the ground during moments of meditative rapture. Yet, he impressed his students less with his supernatural feats than with the fact that he had renounced a very large inheritance.

> "Master, you are wonderful!" A student...gazed ardently at the patriarchal saint. "You have renounced riches and comforts to seek God and teach us wisdom!" It was well known that Bhaduri Mahasaya had forsaken great family wealth in his early childhood, when single-mindedly he had entered the yogic path. "You are reversing the case!" The saint's face held a mild rebuke. "I have left a few paltry, a few petty pleasures, for an empire of cosmic bliss. How then have I denied myself of anything? I know the joy of sharing the treasure. Is that a sacrifice? The shortsighted worldly folk are verily the real renunciants! They renounce an unparalleled divine possession for a poor handful of earthly toys!" (1946, p. 75)

Wordsworth warned that "the world is too much with us; late and soon,/Getting or spending, we lay waste our powers..." (1967, p. 209). This is unfortunately still a relevant caution even to spiritually called teachers as we negotiate our way through a commerce-crazed society and, even more perilously, as we wander through the mazes of our own appetites. Nevertheless, Bhaduri Mahasaya reminds us of what we should be and may become. When teaching attempts—in however great or small a measure, and whatever the subject matter—to convey a sense of the transcendent, how could money, "embodied non-being," ever be a primary motivation? The rewards of teaching from the spirit are many, deep, and lasting. The spiritually called teacher of physics knows this as well as the spiritually called baseball coach. These rewards fill our work with purpose and joy, for we feel that we are having an impact on the lives of our students and our culture. These rewards are literally incalculable; they do not register as dots and slopes of the graphs of disposable income.

Perhaps, then, it is providential that teaching does not pay great financial dividends. If it did, how could the teacher know the temporal opposition without which there is no progression? How could the teacher pass the tests of vocational faith in the commercial wilderness so that his faith might grow fuller? The teacher who works with a sense of ethical mission withstands these trials and deepens his testimony of the eternal because he knows that being a teacher carries a cost. As Dietrich Bonhoeffer, the German pastor who died in the concentration camps, said, true grace is costly. "Cheap grace," on the other hand, is easy to experience but has no power to save (1963). The teacher of "costly grace" attempts to reach his full moral stature and become an example for his students to follow in their own journeys of discovery. This is a refining process that all teachers—even the one who, in my opinion, was the greatest of all—have apparently had to go through in order to fulfill their prophetic calling:

> Again, the devil taketh [Jesus] up into an exceeding high mountain, and sheweth him all the kingdoms of the world, and the glory of them; and saith unto him, All these things will I give thee, if thou wilt fall down and worship me. Then saith Jesus unto him, Get thee hence, Satan, for it is written, Thou shalt worship the Lord they God, and him only shalt thou serve. Then the devil leaveth him, and, behold, angels came and ministered unto him. (Matthew 4: 8-10)

Although few of us are likely to receive visible visitations from angels to minister to us after resisting the seductions of the world, we may well still find that the trial, tempering our faith, has thereby provided its own unique form of comfort.

Renewal and Wonder

A lovely example of the teacher constantly renewing himself in his prophetic role is provided by the psychologist Jeanne Houston in her autobiography, *A Mythic Life.* Here she tells of her first meeting as a girl with a certain teacher-prophet. An adolescent girl then and suffering deeply because of her parents' recent divorce, Houston reports that she was running down 84th Street and Park Avenue in New York City, trying to outstrip her sadness.

> I ran into an old man and knocked the wind out of him. This was serious. I was a great big overgrown girl, and he was a rather frail gentleman in his seventies. But he laughed as I helped him to his feet and asked of me in French-accented speech, "Are you planning to run like that for the rest of your life?" "Yes, sir," I replied, thinking of my unhappiness. "It sure looks that way." "Well, bon voyage!" he said. "Bon voyage!" I answered and sped on my way. (1996, p. 142)

Later, after meeting again in Central Park, they became close friends, regularly strolling the grounds for the next 18 months:

> [H]e was always being carried away by wonder at and astonishment over the simplest things. He was constantly and literally falling in love. I remember one time he fell on his knees in Central Park, his long Gallic nose raking the ground, and exclaimed to me, "Jeanne, look at the caterpillar. Ahhhhh!" I joined him on the ground to see what had provoked so profound a response. "How beautiful it is," he remarked, "this little green being with its wonderful funny little feet. Little furry body, little green feet, on the road to metamorphosis." He then regarded me with interest. "Jeanne, can you feel yourself to be a caterpillar?" "Oh, yes," I replied with the baleful knowing of a gangly, pimply-faced teenager. "Then think of your own metamorphosis," he suggested. "What will you be when you become a butterfly. *Un papillon, eh?*" What is the butterfly of Jeanne?" (1996, p. 142)

Because she didn't speak French, the girl could not quite make out the old gentleman's name on that first day in Central Park but it sounded like "Mr. Thayer," which is what she called him during the year and a half that they met, walked and talked—until one day he simply never showed up again. Yet that relationship not only saw her through the discontented seasons of a troubled adolescence but launched her in directions that would affect her life-vision and life-work. Not until years later as a graduate student did she discover the old man's true identity. Recognizing his photograph on the back of one of her books, *The Phenomenon of Man,* she suddenly realized that the physically slight but spiritually formidable man who had escorted her into new realms of being, was, in fact, one of the towering scholars and teachers of the 20th-century, Teillhard de Chardin, the Jesuit priest, poet, and paleontologist. For Chardin, the teacher-prophet's role as cultural visionary and pioneer of the collective consciousness was inseparable from his ecstatic vision of life itself—"of how we humans are part of an evolutionary process in which we are being drawn toward something he called the Omega Point, the goal of evolution." At the conclusion of what would turn out to be their last meeting, the curious girl asked "Mr. Thayer" her "ultimate question,

> the one that haunted and continues to haunt me all the days of my life. "What do you believe it's all about, Mr. Thayer?" His answer has remained enshrined in my heart. *"Je crois...* I believe that the universe is an evolution. I believe that the evolution is toward Spirit. I believe that the Spirit fulfills itself in a personal god. I believe that the supreme personality is the Universal Christ." "And what do you believe about yourself, Mr. Thayer?" "I believe that I am a pilgrim of the future." (1996, p. 146)

By living in and teaching with this sense of what William James called "ontological wonder," the educator's very being inherently constitutes a challenge to his students' personal prejudices, cultural distortions, and spiritual limitations. From time to time he even transforms or transcends them. Thus he and his students move closer to the beckoning Spirit that is also the alpha and omega of his calling and practice as a teacher.

A Honeycomb Universe

My purpose in this chapter has been to suggest that the teacher may find renewal in a synergy of his spiritual faith and educational practice. Maria Harris (1991), for instance, in her exposition of teaching as incarnation, has drawn upon doctrines, models and images from her Roman Catholicism. Philip Wexler (1996), relying heavily upon his unique interpretation of Kabalistic Judaism, has elaborated his idea of education as an in-gathering of the dispersed sparks of intelligence from their cosmic *diaspora*. Snauwaert (1992) took the *Bhagavad Gita* as a model for the teacher who is attempting to reconcile his personal spiritual conviction with his sense of social responsibility. Needle (1999) constructed his vision of the truly humane educational environment on the six *paramitas* of Buddhism. Tremmel (1993) has mined Zen mindfulness for a wealth of insights into cultivating presence in the classroom with one's students. And I have elsewhere used my commitments as a Latter-day Saint to scaffold my reflectivity as a teacher (Mayes, 2001).

This kind of religious dialogue—well suited to the multifaceted nature of postmodern spirituality—can deepen the teacher's sense of ontological wonder. Such conversations about what different spiritual perspectives have to offer us as spiritually called teachers need not imply relativism. It does not require the teacher to abandon or "mythologize" his core commitments. Rather, it recognizes the inevitable and healthy fact that whatever the ultimate nature of things (if there *is* an ultimate nature of things), we live in a universe of many different chambers, passages, twists, turns, and destinations—a honeycomb universe, James's "pluralistic universe."

Recently, the transpersonal psychologist and theorist Jorge Ferrer has introduced the term "enactive spirituality" to capture this reality. Enactive spirituality not only affirms the *subjective* validity of many forms of transpersonal experience but goes a step farther to make the broader point that those multiple forms may each have its own distinct but valid form of *ontological reality*—one that embraces all of those individuals who are joined in a particular community of belief. This goes well beyond the comfortable but simplistic notion that there are many paths up the mountain—some strictly personal and others formal—but that they all ultimately get you to the very same destination. Ferrer's vision is much more nuanced than that. For him, reality is a mountain with many different peaks, not just one. Or in Ferrer's words, it is possible that

> *the various traditions lead to enactment of different spiri-*
> *tual ultimates and/or transconceptual disclosures of reality.*
> Although these spiritual ultimates may share some quali-
> ties..., they constitute independent religious aims whose
> conflation may prove to be a serious mistake.... *We could*
> *say, then, that the Ocean of Emancipation has many shores.*
> (2002, p. 147)

It is not so much that there are many *roads to* salvation as that
there may be many different *kinds of* salvation—corresponding roughly
to what in my religion are called different "kingdoms" (*Doctrine and*
Covenants of the Church of Jesus Christ of Latter-day Saints, 86).

If Ferrer's hypothesis is correct, then it is highly desirable for the
spiritually committed teacher who wishes to remain in dialogue with
other faith-perspectives to maintain a dynamic equipoise between
"commitment and openness" (Simmer-Brown, 1999, p. 97). In doing
so, spiritually called teachers may reflect Mr. Thayer's ever ancient,
ever new sense of ontological wonder—may communicate it *to* and
cultivate it *in* their students, just as Chardin did with Jeanne. The rip-
ples in the students' souls from those instructional pebbles may spread
through their lifetimes.

The Bow and the All

When the German philosopher Eugene Herrigel traveled to Japan
to study the art of archery at a Zen monastery in Tokyo, one of the first
lessons that he learned from the Zen monk who became his teacher was
that "when drawn to its full extent, the bow encloses the 'All' in itself"
(1971, p. 20). So in their respective fields, whether industrial arts or literature, spiritually called teachers discover and provide access to the
many universes that are contained in what they teach. For it is precisely
through *that particular subject* that the Divine Voice called the teacher
to teach in the first place. Of course, each teacher combines the vibra-
tions of his own voice with those of the transcendent One, but he does
so in a way that is faithful to his calling and allows him to mature in
that calling. Teaching then becomes a constant occasion for ontological
growth. It becomes a perpetual point of departure on an eternal journey
into endless ways of seeing and being.

In this process, teachers do not relinquish their authoritative role in
the classroom, but neither do they autocratically insist on agreement or
deference. Through the medium of their subject matter, they illustrate

that the universe is a "whole spectrum of interwoven levels of being" (Hayward, 1999, p. 67). Without succumbing to the easy fixes of either syncretism or relativism, they cultivate in both themselves and their students an ability to "rest in the ambiguity of religious difference" (Simmer-Brown, 1999, p. 101). Teacher and student thus "find ways to research the world by occupying the other's viewpoint" (Palmer, 1983, p. 116). The result is delight at the endlessness of ontological variety— a delight that is at the heart of viable spirituality and vibrant spiritual teaching.

Topics for Discussion

The author insists that the teacher not only accept but embrace the misunderstanding of others regarding his decision to teach, for it will provide the necessary opposition to strengthen his sense of calling. Some have argued that this position results in political passivity that keeps the teacher from fighting to eliminate misunderstandings and gain greater financial and social rewards. However, the counterargument is that if teachers begin to gain substantial financial and social rewards, then people may start entering the profession because of its benefits and status (as has happened in law, medicine and other high-prestige professions), not because of a true sense of calling to serve children in the schools. Where do you stand on this complex issue? Is there perhaps some middle ground to be discovered?

Is it realistic to expect teachers in today's public schools to cultivate and communicate "ontological wonder" about their subjects when they have to labor under so many legal, institutional, and curricular constraints? Some argue that it is not only realistic but necessary if teachers are to survive with their dignity and sense of mission intact. Others argue that it is impossible. What is your opinion?

Topics for Research

Review the literature on "teacher renewal." What are some of the major theories and practices about how to help teachers rediscover the emotional and ethical wellsprings of their calling? What could a site-based leader at a school do to help his or her staff engage in such practices and put them into practical action in the classroom?

Topics for Research (continued)

Read the section entitled "Curriculum as a Theological Text" in Pinar and his associates' (1995) book, *Understanding Curriculum.* How has postmodern religious dialogue informed certain views of curriculum and instruction? Does the postmodern view of spirituality represented in this text harmonize or conflict with your understanding of spirituality? How, if at all, do the readings in this section affect your views about the pedagogical implications of your personal spiritual commitments?

Four

An Intuitive Pedagogy

Living and Teaching in "Habitual Intuition"

Daisetzu Suzuki, the world-renowned interpreter of Zen Buddhism to the West, was once asked by an American college student to define "enlightenment." The monk quickly replied that no such definition was possible. Enlightenment transcended propositional discourse. The student asked again, and Suzuki politely repeated that he could not offer such a definition. Undaunted, the student asked a third time. Suzuki sighed and told the young man that by asking a question three times he had, according to an unwritten Buddhist pedagogical law, laid Suzuki as a teacher under the obligation of at least attempting an answer. Drawing a deep breath and smiling gently, Suzuki replied that enlightenment was the state of living in "habitual intuition." In this chapter, I would like to explore some of the ways in which spiritual teaching involves habitual intuition.

In *The Varieties of Religious Experience,* William James (1902) observed that in both the Eastern and Western traditions "it is a commonplace of metaphysics that God's knowledge cannot be discursive but must be intuitive, that is, must be constructed more after the pattern of what in ourselves is called immediate feeling than after that of proposition and judgment" (p. 311). It should not be surprising, then, that for the spiritually called teacher, propositional truth, although undoubtedly important and often the heart of classroom discourse, must nevertheless exist in the broader context of the teacher's and student's intuitive sense of the transcendent. For, this is the source from which the teacher's calling issues and to which it returns. In this way, the teacher and student may experience for themselves the truth of the statement that "the course of the Lord is one eternal round" (*Book of Mormon* 1 Nephi 10: 19), where the end is always a higher beginning for a new evolutionary ring in an eternally expanding spiral. In Kantian terms, no matter how "mathetic" (or propositional) the subject-matter is, the spiritually called teacher apprehends and conveys it to her students largely through "poetic" (or intuitive) modes. Seen in this light, therefore, teaching is largely a "poetic" art, not a "mathetic" technology. This is why technique-based forms of teacher education are untrue to the intuitive nature of teaching.

When Eugene Herrigel left his academic position and took up a six-year residence in Tokyo to study archery, it was precisely because the propositional approach to truth had not answered his fundamental questions and needs. Nevertheless, the single-minded devotion to reason did not yield easily in Herrigel. When the Zen master who was Herrigel's teacher pointed out the need for this inner change before any outward manifestations in archery could occur, the frustrated student responded (in very telling imagery), "that is just what I cannot get *in my head!"*

> "I think I understand what you mean by the real inner goal which ought to be hit. But how it happens that the outer goal, the disk of paper, is hit without the archer's taking aim, and that the hits are only outward confirmations of inner events, that correspondence is beyond me." "You are under an illusion," said the Master after awhile, "if you imagine that even a rough understanding of these dark connections would help you. These are processes that are beyond the reach of understanding." (1971, p. 32-33)

The Master does not mean that these processes negate or even minimize reason; they simply go *beyond* it in such a way that they place it in its proper, secondary role. Drawing on Yogic epistemology, this might be called teaching and learning with the third eye. To see and teach one's subject in this way requires the teacher to develop certain transcendent qualities. Sri Yukteswar explained to Yogananda that

> "unlike the spatial, three-dimensional physical world cog-
> nized only by the five senses, the astral spheres are visible
> to the all inclusive sixth sense—intuition." Sri Yukteswar
> went on, "By sheer intuitional feeling, all astral beings see,
> hear, smell, taste and touch. They possess three eyes, two
> of which are partly closed. The third and chief astral eye,
> vertically placed on the forehead, is open." (1946, p. 481)

Similarly (even if symbolically) the spiritually called teacher views his
subject matter spiritually. Brigham Young once told Dr. Karl Maeser, a
very influential teacher in early Mormon history, that a teacher should
not even teach the multiplication table except by the Spirit of God.

To teach spiritually therefore requires that the teacher constantly
work at developing her intuitive capacity—in how she relates to both
her subject-matter and students. Using the metaphor of the eye in a
slightly different way but to the same purpose, Parker Palmer (1983)
reminds teachers who want to teach in the spirit that

> many of us live one-eyed lives. We rely largely on the eye
> of the mind to form our image of reality. But today more
> and more of us are opening the other eye, the eye of the
> heart, looking for realities to which the mind's eye is blind.
> Either eye alone is not enough. We need "wholesight," a
> vision of the world in which mind and heart unite, "as my
> two eyes make one in sight." Our seeing shapes our being.
> Only as we see whole can we and our world be whole. (p.
> xi)

Teaching with the third eye, teaching with "wholesight"—it is fas-
cinating how the symbol of the eye pervades the literature on intuitive
teaching. Yet another variation on this theme comes from Don Juan,
who talks, in his typically comic but ultimately serious way, of seeing,
learning and teaching "cross-eyed." Don Juan is instructing Castaneda
about how to find his *sitio* or "location of power." In Buddhist meditation, the master will also sometimes talk about the importance of finding one's "seat." This is both a physical and spiritual locale, the existentially and spatially centered point from which the student learns to
see and respond to the flow of events with efficiency and compassion.
But one cannot reason oneself in the direction of this spot. It takes intuition to find it.

After a long pause Don Juan suddenly turned to me and
said that in order to find the proper place to rest all I had to
do was to cross my eyes. He gave me a knowing look and
in a confidential tone told me that I had done precisely that
when I was rolling on his porch.... "I really don't know
what I did," I said. "You crossed your eyes," he said em-
phatically. "That's the technique; you must have done that,
although you don't remember it." Don Juan then described
the technique, which he said took years to perfect, and
which consisted of gradually forcing the eyes to see sepa-
rately the same image. This lack of image conversion en-
tailed *a double perception of the world*; this double perception, according to Don Juan, allowed one the opportunity of
judging changes in the surroundings, which the eyes were
ordinarily incapable of perceiving. (Castaneda, 1972, p. 72.
Emphasis added)

Never neglecting the inherent importance of the subject matter and
rationally exploring it, the spiritual teacher views it not as an end in itself but ultimately as an ontological doorway into an intuitive appre-
hension of the spirit. With their newly acquired "double perception" of
the subject matter as temporal and spiritual, students may now pass into
a higher plane of existence. The essential evil of much standardized
testing is that it autocratically interrogates the student about artificially
isolated bits of subject-matter but ignores—and covertly attempts to de-
stroy—education's more important job of feeding the spirit. It forces
student and teacher alike, in a terrible act of pedagogical self-
immolation, to gouge the third eye so that they will have to follow programs of domination blindly.

Passing the Mantle On
Through ongoing acts of purification and commitment in the refining fires of teaching, the teacher finds ways to resist corporate domination, helping students challenge the various powers that would suppress
their spirits. When the teacher finds the spirit by intuition, she commu-
nicates that spirit to her students through the general medium of intuition—and in the specific form of subject matter. Then the student, having touched the divine through the teacher and the subject, embarks on
the journey that sometimes results in her becoming a teacher, too. And
so the chain remains unbroken, and the relationship between the teacher

and student is the ever ancient, ever new affirmation of life—and of the life beyond this life. The intuitive passing down of the pedagogical mantle from teacher to student is central in the literature on spiritual teaching. "Sri Yukteswar taught me how to summon the blessed experience at will," confides Yogananda, "and also how to transmit it to others when their intuitive channels are developed" (1946, p. 171):

> "Do you want the whole divine *chana* (milk curd) for yourself alone?" My guru's retort was accompanied by a stern glance. "Could you, or anyone else, achieve God-communion through yoga if a line of generous-hearted masters had not been willing to convey their knowledge to others?" He added, "God is the Honey, organizations are the hives. Any form is useless, of course, without the spirit, but why should you not start busy hives [which would later become Yogananda's schools and ashrams] full of the spiritual nectar." His counsel moved me deeply. Although I made no outward reply, an adamant resolution arose in my breast. I would share with my fellows, so far as lay in my power, the unshackling truths I had learned at my guru's feet. (Yogananda, 1946, p. 287)

In this way, the divine voice echoes down time in the various resonances within the teachers it touches. In reverence of this fact, Don Juan instructed Castaneda that "[t]here is power in the bones of a warrior..., and there is even more power in the bones of a man of knowledge." Like the Hindu guru, the Yaqui holy man is a link in the spiritual chain of instruction.

> "I'm a hunter," [Don Juan] said, as if he were reading my thoughts. "I leave very little to chance. Perhaps I should explain to you that I learned to be a hunter. I have not always lived the way I do now. At one point in my life I had to change. Now I'm pointing the direction to you. I'm guiding you. I know what I'm talking about; someone taught me all this. I didn't figure it out for myself." "Do you mean that you had a teacher, Don Juan?" "Let's say that someone taught me how to hunt the way I want to teach you now," he said and quickly changed the topic. (Castaneda, 1972, p. 79)

Intuiting the Holy

The spiritual teacher—truly a fellow-traveler with students in an endless cosmic odyssey—aids them in their vision-quest by helping them develop their "intuitive channels" regarding a particular subject. The literature on spiritual instruction offers many examples of how teachers do this. Even in the most analytical disciplines, the teacher's use of literary devices and dramatic strategies is frequently essential to instruction that engages not only the student's head but also her heart.

For instance, when Black Elk, the great 19th-century Ogalala medicine man, tells his biographer, John Niehardt, about the vision that began his career as a holy man of his nation, he at first does so not in great specificity but in such ethereal terms as to allow Niehardt to catch "a vision of the vision" for himself. For like most teacher-prophets, Black Elk knows that the awakening of the divine in the student, being an "event" both in and out of time, must use not only time's direct language but also the intuitive grammar of eternity. Thus, the spiritual teacher of physics as well as of dance must ultimately rest in and return to poetic ways of knowing and communicating. It is said that Einstein first conceived of the theory of relativity as a poetic image when as a boy he wondered what it would be like to ride a beam of light. In any spiritually oriented pedagogy, the goal is transcendence; and what transcends time also transcends language, although discourse and reason can sometimes help point the way.

Black Elk knew all of this at the tender age of nine years old, when he was vouchsafed his vision—one that, in my view, is perhaps equaled in the apocalyptic literature only by the Revelation to St. John on the Island of Patmos in its cosmic power and scope. To be sure, Black Elk later offers a much more specific narrative of the shamanistic journey on which he was taken throughout the universe as initiation into his sacred role as the tribal priest. Nevertheless, the core of the experience is, and will always remain, just that—an *experience*. It cannot be adequately rendered by the paltry, tinny tokens of merely human language. When he was a boy, Black Elk recalls, he "would try to make words for the meaning [of his tour of the universe, but] it would be like fog and get away from me." Lest, however, the reader think that this ineffability was the function of a boy's limited linguistic power, Black Elk immediately goes on to claim that even as an adult:

It was the pictures I remembered and the [sacred, heavenly] words that went with them; for nothing I have ever seen with my eyes was so clear and bright as what my vision showed me; and no words that I have ever heard with my ears were like the words I heard.... It was as I grew older that the meanings came clearer and clearer out of the pictures and the words; and even now I know that more was shown to me than I can tell. (Black Elk, 1932, p. 49)

Black Elk later speaks as well of the vision of his cousin, Crazy Horse, that endued him with the right and power to become the chief of their tribe; and again we learn that the only passport into the land of ultimate reality is written in the language of eternity and stamped with the seal of intuition. Our shadow language simply cannot describe the contours of the sacred landscape, as Black Elk suggests when he says that Crazy Horse "went into the world where there is nothing but the spirits of things. That is the real world that is behind this one, and everything we see here is something like a shadow from that world" (Black Elk, 1932, p. 85).

The East offers many examples of what Chuangtse, the third-century B.C.E. Taoist sage, called "teaching the doctrine with no words" (Yutang, 1946). This form of spiritual pedagogy, with its emphasis of imagery, intuition, and moral action, is central to instruction in the Zen Buddhist tradition. The Trappist monk and poet Thomas Merton said of the Zen way of teaching that "the language is *not metaphysical* but poetic and phenomenological..." (1967, p. 20). In *Zen and the Art of Archery,* Herrigel, having briefly experienced a state of grace in his shooting, is now open to the higher message of which "the curriculum of his bow" was primarily (and in this case *literally*) an instrument. Having helped the student apprehend the divine *in* the subject, the teacher ultimately leads the student *beyond* the subject. This is the paradox that lies at the very center of spiritual teaching. The teacher deals with subject matter, and this subject matter is important, but its ultimate importance is that it is a springboard into eternity. A teacher's teaching (whether about archery or history) includes but transcends a particular curricular domain.

Contenting himself with a few practice shots, the Master went on to expound the "Great Doctrine" in relation to the art of archery, and to adapt it to the stage we had reached.

Although *he dealt in mysterious images and dark compari-sons,* the meagerest hints were sufficient for us to under-stand what it was all about. He dwelt longest on the "artless art" which must be the goal of archery if it is to reach per-fection. "He who can shoot with the horn of the hare and the hair of the tortoise and can hit the center without bow (horn) and arrow (hair), he alone is Master in the highest sense of the word—Master of the artless art. Indeed, he is the artless art itself and thus Master and no-Master in one. At this point, archery, considered as the unmoved move-ment, the undanced dance, passes over into Zen." (1971, p. 73. Emphasis added)

The teacher, the taught, the subject, and the site—Schwabb's four famous curricular "commonplaces"—are now shot through with divin-ity in the trajectory of an arrow. "Now at last," says Herrigel's master, "the bowstring has cut right through you."

A student often comes to class expecting to learn a set body of "es-tablished" facts and theories that she must reproduce on a test. But this is not what happens in the spiritual classroom, where the teacher uses intuition, indirection, complexity, humor and paradox to problematize the subject-matter and defamiliarize the student's convenient "reali-ties." The student comes expecting external information—but the teacher requires internal transformation; she requires the student to be "cut through" by the "bowstring" of the curriculum as the *sine qua non* of moral and spiritual growth.

This is precisely the problem that Don Juan faces in his tutelage of Castaneda, who wants to reduce and record his experiences with a holy man into a set of filed field notes. As is so often the case in Native American teaching, Don Juan uses stories, parables, poetry, and humor to radicalize Castaneda's world and thus shake him out of his spiritual slumber. In order to turn the plodding social scientist into a potent shaman, Don Juan must awaken the young man to the Mystery which surrounds and beckons him. And it should be noted that, in this sense, spiritual teaching is fundamentally an act of prayer. For like prayer, spiritual teaching should "[bring] us to the edge of a great mystery where we become inarticulate, where our knowledge fails" (Palmer, 1983, p. 125). Don Juan tells Castaneda, "we are in a weird world, you know." I nodded my head affirmatively. "We're not talking about the same thing," he said. "For you the world is weird because if you're not bored with it you're at odds with it. For me the world is weird because it is stupendous, awesome, mysterious, unfathomable; my interest has been to convince you that you must assume responsibility for being here, in this marvelous world, this marvelous desert, at this marvelous time." (1972, p. 107)

Don Juan's instruction is prayerful. It aims to lead Castaneda to the humble recognition of the Mystery not only that he is *in* but also the Mystery that he *is*. Hence in Don Juan's desert classroom of shrubs, hills and cactuses, the very language of instruction must be the prayerful language of mystery: "There are certain things we will talk about from now on only at places of power," Don Juan tells the puzzled young anthropologist. "I have brought you here because this is your first trial. This is a place of power, and here we can talk only about power" (1972, p. 125).

The spiritual teacher draws on a wide variety of poetic devices to stimulate the student's intuitive ability to discover new dimensions of the Spirit. She helps students explore both subject-matter and themselves in ways that are ultimately poetic. The result is transcendence of self and subject—or rather, the inclusion of self and subject in that greater Reality which is at once the ground and goal of the teacher's and student's being. At its spiritual best, the discourse of the classroom—whether the classroom is a high-tech university classroom or a parched arroyo in the Sonora desert—is a venture in intuition and a form of prayer.

Topics for Discussion

Is there a teacher in your experience as a student who you feel was important in opening you up to intuitive ways of thinking about the subject-matter in her classroom? Has that influence continued in any form throughout your life?

How might you go about developing a deeper intuitive understanding of what you teach and the people to whom you teach it? In answer-

Topics for Discussion (continued)

ing this question, you might want to consider such things as journal writing, painting, poetry, and other explorative activities that could aid you in your process.

Have you ever had a teacher who was particularly good at using humor in her teaching? Was her humor a way of leading you to deeper insights into your subject-matter? If so, how did she do this with certain specific ideas or topics?

Are there some fields or topics for which intuition as a primary mode of exploration and analysis might be less suitable than others?

Topics for Research

Read *Transpersonal Education: A Curriculum for Feeling and Being* by Hendricks and Fadminan (1976), *Getting It All Together: Confluent Education* by Brown, Phillips, and Shapiro (1976), and *Psychosynthesis in Education: A Guide to the Joy of Learning* by Whitmore (1986). Discuss their ideas and approaches for enlarging students' understanding of subject-matter through awakening their intuitive understanding of it. Also, discuss how you might use some of those ideas given the level and/or subject-matter that you teach or plan to teach? Comment, as well, on the general appropriateness (or inappropriateness) of intuitive approaches with regard to your specific level and/or subject-matter.

Critically examine and write a review of Schön's influential work *Educating the Reflective Practitioner* (1987), in which he talks about the dangers of "technical rationality" and the need to honor intuition in educating practitioners such as architects, doctors, lawyers, teachers, and others.

Look at Carl Jung's classic (1921) study, *Psychological Types*. In that work, Jung claimed that there are four different, basic ways in which individuals tend to register and portray their experience. He suggested that these correspond to what he believed were the four basic

Topics for Research (continued)

personality types: intuitive, thinking, sensate, and feeling. Examine these four personality types in depth in Jung's study in order to gain a deeper conceptual grasp of the nature and dynamics of each personality type. The famous Myers-Briggs test, which analyzes and portrays one's personality along these four dimensions, is based on Jung's original research. If possible, take this test to see which personality type best characterizes you. Then, on the basis of your study of Jung and your own test results, write a response paper in which you examine the thesis of this chapter that the intuitive mode is the one best suited to spiritually based teaching. Do you agree or disagree with this? Can you imagine some ways in which this typological knowledge may be helpful to you in enhancing your effectiveness as a spiritually committed teacher?

Five

Pedagogy, Relationship and the Miraculous

Pure Dialogue

Crucial to any spiritual teaching is fully engaged dialogue between the teacher and student. By dialogue I mean more than simply lively conversation although that is certainly part of it. Dialogue as I want to use the word implies a worldview that honors the basic need and duty to relate to other people in ways that are intellectually and emotionally honest and compassionate. Martin Buber (1985) saw relationship as both the basis and goal of any deeply educational situation, for "the relation in education is one of pure dialogue." He also claimed that such relationships were the cornerstone of morality. Hence, he made "dialogical ethics" the foundation of his pedagogy. For Buber, teaching, relationship, and religion are ultimately indistinguishable from each other. "The extended lines of relation meet in the eternal *Thou*," wrote Buber in his classic work *I and Thou*, and

> every particular *Thou* is a glimpse through to the eternal *Thou;* by means of every particular *Thou*, the primary word addresses the eternal *Thou*. Through the mediation of the *Thou* of all beings, fulfillment, and non-fulfillment, of relations comes to them: The inborn *Thou* is realized in each relation and consummated in none. (Buber, 1965, p. 75)

Buber contrasted the "primary word" of *I-Thou* with the other primary word, *I-it.* An *I-it* relationship is destructive, for the "I" in this dyad has no interest in exploring or empowering the other person as a unique "Thou" with eternal potential. Instead, the "I" of the *I-it* relationship, seeing the other person as an object of its own selfish desires and goals, tries to negate the other's existential identity and spiritual needs in order to feed its own insatiable appetite and will. Yet because we gain access to the sacred only to the degree that we respond to it in others, we close the door on divinity whenever we "objectify" another person in any fashion.

Thus it is imperative that the spiritual teacher enter into a relationship with the student in an ever deeper moral encounter. The subject under analysis in the classroom is the curricular scaffolding for this ethical process—a process that *illuminates* subject matter but ultimately *transcends* it as the teacher and student, through dialogical encounter, approach the light of the divine. In this sense, education is a form of prayer, as Palmer has asserted in his call for "a mode of knowing and educating that is prayerful through and through. What do I mean by prayer? I mean the practice of relatedness." Prayerful teaching implies "allowing the power of love to transform the very knowledge we teach, the very methods we use to teach and learn it" (Palmer, 1983, p. 10). "The living mystery of life is always hidden between Two, and it is the true mystery which cannot be betrayed by words and depleted by arguments" (Jung as cited in Marshak, 1998, p. 58). Whatever sets itself up against relationship in education does moral violence. It also does intellectual violence because the teacher and student will achieve the most profound forms of understanding of the subject matter by exploring it together.

Educational scenarios such as those defined in the Reagan administration's *A Nation at Risk* report, which considers "the basic purposes of schooling" to be primarily the reestablishment of America's "once unchallenged preeminence in commerce, industry, science, and technological innovation," work against the spirit in education. They measure the teacher and student in the clinically anonymous language of psychometrics. Von Clausewitz said that war is the extension of national policy by military means. In these corporate visions of reform, teaching is the extension of national policy by *educational* means. Thus, the dean of American educational historians, Laurence Cremin, has warned that the military-industrial complex is rapidly morphing into a military-industrial-*educational* complex, with the direst consequences for democracy—a political system which, as Dewey always insisted, rests upon a public education system that is free to critique the existing order, not to slavishly serve it.

This is not to assert that education may not have personally and economically practical purposes. In fact, most parents probably expect teachers to arm children with pragmatic skills and knowledge that will help them survive in the marketplace. This is an understandable and necessary consideration in a postindustrial society. But when such purposes become the centerpiece of a national agenda—vaunting themselves as "the basic purposes of education" virtually to the exclusion of anything else—then education is being ordered to grovel in worship of the god of the Bottom-Line. I am convinced that this is the primary cause of many teachers' disillusionment with and abandonment of American public education. Most teachers' sense of calling grows out of the primary word *I-Thou*—out of their need to engage, excite, nurture and shape the burgeoning hearts and minds of their young students. But corporate reform agendas grow out of the primary word *I-it* in their ceaseless attempt to create and control markets. As Marx saw, this is ultimately a psychosocial project whose unspoken but omnipresent motivation is the objectification of its members. In this manner, people are increasingly conditioned not only to be *addicted* to commodities but to *become* commodities. Here is the false god of *I-it* triumphant, a fiscal deity who commands schools to become sites of commercial training and conditioning—to become places, in short, where teachers and students are treated (and so come to treat each other) as objects. This is what Marx called "commodity fetishism" in a particularly insidious pedagogical form (1978).

The single antidote to this psychosocial illness in its many manifestations is the *I-Thou* relationship, and in few instances is the antidote more effective than in the educational relationship. Where teachers and students maintain and nurture ways of learning and growing together within the sacred precinct of *I-Thou* they are engaged in a spiritual act of political resistance. The teacher's vocation is to remind her students (and thus ultimately her people) that "if a man lets it have the mastery, the continuing growing world of *It* overruns him and robs him of the reality of his own *I*, till the incubus over him and the ghost within him whisper to one another the confession of their non-salvation" (Buber, 1965, p. 46). The aim of spiritual education is nothing less than psychic, social, and spiritual redemption and reformation—and it is a goal that can be accomplished insofar as the educative relationship brings teacher and student—through the medium of curriculum and the intensity of mutuality—into a deepening involvement with each other and, thus, the divine.

The Classroom as a Temenos

Even the gruff Yaqui medicine man Don Juan occasionally reveals his tenderness regarding his dense student. After a trying set of spiritual exercises in which Castaneda came off looking the fool, the young man felt

> an overwhelming loneliness. I expressed my feelings of sadness. [Don Juan] smiled. His fingers gently clasped the top of my hand. "We both are beings who are going to die," he said softly.... His touch was firm and friendly; it was like a reassurance that he was concerned and had affection for me, and at the same time it gave me the impression of an unwavering purpose.... "This is my gesture for you," he said, holding the grip he had on my hand for an instant. "Now you must go by yourself into those friendly mountains." He pointed with his chin to the distant range of mountains towards the southeast. (1972, p. 92)

The deeper the psychospiritual ties between the master and the student, the more attuned both grow to each other's deepest feelings. In Paramahansa Yogananda's case, this resulted in one of the many supernatural occurrences that peppered his life.

> About eight-thirty on Wednesday morning, a telepathic message from Sri Yukteswar flashed insistently to my mind: "I am delayed. Don't meet the nine o'clock train...."
> As the room was rather dark, I moved nearer to a window overlooking the street. The scant sunlight suddenly increased to an intense brilliancy in which the iron-barred window completely vanished. Against this dazzling background appeared the clearly materialized figure of Sri Yukteswar. Bewildered to the point of shock, I rose from my chair and knelt before him.... "I was pleased that you got my telepathic message." Master's voice was calm, entirely normal. "I have now finished my business in Calcutta, and shall arrive in Serampore by the ten o'clock train...." (1946, pp. 216-217)

The teacher does not have to be a great saint or mystic to have out-of-the-ordinary experiences. At least once each term, I find that as my relationship with a class quickens, some sort of extraordinary event occurs. For me, this usually happens as a synchronistic sequence of events. Carl Jung, the great Swiss psychotherapist who introduced the term synchronicity, also called it "acausal connectedness" to indicate when two or more events are connected in a meaningful pattern (usually involving proximity in time) but where there is virtually no possibility that one could have "caused" the other in any ordinary physical sense.

> As Rhine's ESP (extrasensory perception) experiments show, any intense emotional interest or fascination is accompanied by phenomena which can only be explained by a psychic relativity of time, space, and causality.... [Synchronistic phenomena] consist in the *meaningful* coincidence of two or more causally unrelated facts. (Jung, 1973, p. 184, fn. 1)

For example, let us say that I dream of a student whom I have not seen or heard from in 20 years—and one whom I have never dreamt of before. The next day, completely out of the blue, he strolls into my office, entirely unannounced. My dream did not *cause* his visit. Nor could his visit have caused my dream (at least not by any traditional space-time models). That the events are *meaningfully connected* is clear—but that connection is not of the ordinary causal variety. It is *acausal.* This suggests that a power that transcends our ordinary space-time limitations has orchestrated the correspondence. This is what gives such experiences a mysterious aura—*numinosity* as Jung called it.

Jung often experienced synchronicity in the consulting room when the therapeutic relationship with the patient became especially intense. He said that these relationally "electric" situations contain such potent energy that they generate a special, psychically super-charged space that he called a *temenos,* or "sacred precinct" (Jung, 1956, 1959, 1963). Wherever there is the possibility of a deeply transformative relationship (such as the consulting room or the classroom), there is also a potential *temenos.* Some Jungians even make the intriguing claim that the image of a *temenos* in such places as the consulting room, the meditation hall, the field of battle, the classroom, and any other area where intense relationships are forming, is more than merely symbolic. It may—as certain recent investigations suggest—involve the actual generation of psychophysical energies that form a quantum field which forms a fertile ground for the emergence of synchronistic phenomena (Schwartz-Salant, 1995; Spiegelmann, 1996). As unusual as this psychophysical claim is, there is a growing body of evidence to suggest that it is true (Brennan, 1988; Spiegelman, 1996). Jung's term "sacred precinct" may be more literally descriptive than even he imagined. Let me give just a few examples of many such experiences that I have had in my 25 years of teaching that have led me to believe this claim.

Last term I dreamed that I was singing Beethoven's "Ode to Joy" in German with a student. This student, Mark, was emerging as a leader in a cohort that was just beginning to come together as a group. He and I were about the same age and I felt a particularly strong bond with him. When I told the students about my dream the following day so that we could all have a good laugh out of the image of Mark and me singing Beethoven at the top of our lungs, everyone did laugh—everyone, that is, except Mark. When he heard the dream, his mouth dropped open and he went a little pale. When I asked him why, he told me that last night he had been trying to learn how to read music on the guitar and had been practicing by repeatedly playing the famous *Freude, schöne Götterfunken* theme from Beethoven's "Ode to Joy."

Another example stems from a discussion that I was having three years ago with a class regarding the idea of synchronicity itself. I was illustrating the idea of synchronicity by telling this graduate seminar about a very impressive synchronicity I had experienced several years before involving a book and a white dog. As has often been my experience when speaking about synchronicity to classes, I could see that this class politely but clearly wanted to dismiss the story (the details of which are not important here) as mere fantasy on my part. There was one lone student, however, Paula, who bravely raised her hand and said that her classmates should not reject the idea of synchronicity so cavalierly (as my religiously conservative students were inclined to do) because she often had such experiences herself. Amidst a chorus of good-humored jibes from her fellow classmates that she was just "brown-nosing," she stood her ground and said that such phenomena were possible if one was open to them. The next day as class began, Paula shyly raised her hand. She said that the previous night after class, she had driven directly home. Getting out of her car, she opened the mailbox and found a book inside that had been placed there by someone in a reading circle of which she was a member. The book, which she had never seen or heard of before, was entitled *The White Dog* and had a picture of a large white dog on its cover. She felt (quite rightly, I believe) that this was a cosmic validation of her courageous stand in class.

What Buber would call the "pure dialogue" which these students and I were engaged in had created a psychospiritually charged field which encompassed us all. This pedagogical space, this classroom *temenos,* shaped by powerful emotional forces and rich with educational possibilities, is a testimony to the educational power of the primal word *I-Thou.*

Where the World Ends

The spiritually focused teacher's relationship with her student can be so great that in some remarkable cases it has even traversed the grave and bridged planes of being. We feel the abiding nature of this transtemporal bond in the touching scene where Herrigel takes leave of his Zen master after six years of study.

> In farewell, and yet not in farewell, the Master handed me his best bow. "When you shoot with this bow, you will feel the spirit of the Master near you. Give it not into the hands of the curious! And when you have passed beyond it, do not lay it up in remembrance! Destroy it, so that nothing remains but a heap of ashes." (1971, p. 74)

Paramahansa Yogananda reported a more literal reunion with his guru, Sri Yukteswar, after that teacher's passing. This astonishing autobiographical event bears citing at length.

> Sitting on my bed at the Bombay hotel at three o'clock in the afternoon of June 19, 1936..., I was roused from my meditation by a beatific light. Before my open and astonished eyes, the whole room was transformed into a strange world, the sunlight transmuted into supernal splendor. Waves of rapture engulfed me as I beheld the flesh and blood form of Sri Yukteswar! "My son!" Master spoke tenderly, on his face an angel-bewitching smile. For the first time in my life I did not kneel at his feet, but instantly advanced to gather him hungrily in my arms. Moment of moments! The anguish of past months was toll I counted weightless against the torrential bliss now descending.... "But is it *you,* Master, the same Lion of God? Are you wearing a body like the one I buried beneath cruel Puri sands?" "Yes, my child, I am the same. Though I see [my

body] as ethereal, to your sight it is physical...." "Adorable Master, please tell me more about the astral cosmos." Though I had slightly relaxed my embrace at Sri Yukteswar's request, my arms were still around him. Treasure beyond all treasures, my guru who had laughed at death to reach me." (1946, p. 475-481)

Even after his passing, there were many credible reports that Sri Yukteswar continued to be a teacher to Yogananda—just as Yogananda, almost 50 years after *his* passing, is said to visit and instruct some of his most faithful disciples today—as I was personally informed several years ago during a conversation with a head monk of one of Yogananda's ashrams who intimated to me and my wife that he had received a post-mortal visit from his beloved Yogananda.

Black Elk was also instructed by teachers who spoke from the other side of the grave. He begins his apocalyptic account in his "Great Vision" by recalling:

> I could see out through the opening [of his parents' tepee], and there two men were coming from the clouds, head-first, like arrows slanting down.... Each...carried a long spear, and from the points of these a jagged lightning flashed. They came clear down to the ground at this time and stood a little way off and looked at me and said, "Hurry! Come! Your Grandfathers are calling you!" Then they turned and left the ground like arrows slanting upward from the bow. I went outside the tepee and yonder where the men with flaming spears were going, a little cloud was coming very fast. It came and stooped and took me and turned back to where it came from, flying fast.... Then there was nothing but the air and the swiftness of the little cloud that bore me and those two men still leading up to where white clouds were piled like mountains on a wide blue plain, and in them thunder beings lived and leaped and flashed. (Black Elk, 1932, p. 22)

To the spiritually called teacher this sort of thing should come as no great surprise, for she knows that the call comes from an eternal domain and ultimately returns to it—there to develop in endless rounds of evolution.

One of my favorite Latter-day Saint hymns also deals, like Sri Yukteswar's post-mortal lesson to Yogananda, with a journey to a place inhabited by divine beings. Significantly for us as teachers, this heavenly journey also results in a message about eternal progression through eternal learning:

> There is no end to virtue,
> There is no end to might,
> There is no end to wisdom,
> There is no end to light.
> (*Hymns of the Church of Jesus Christ of Latter-day Saints,*
> # 284)

With Paul, the spiritually called teacher declares from the heart of her vocation, "O death, where is thy sting? O grave, where is thy victory?" (1 Corinthians 15:55). And with all of the master spiritual-teachers whom she loves and tries to emulate, the spiritual teacher is always open to the breaking-through of the miraculous in her classroom.

Accompanying the Student-Heroine on Her Road of Trials

The sincerity of the teacher's care inspires trust in the student, who comes to believe that it is now safe to venture into new intellectual and spiritual territory because she has a guide and friend—perhaps for the first time in her life. In archetypal terms, the time is ripe for the emergence of the teacher in the archetypal form of the Wise Old Man or Wise Old Woman. With this person, the archetypal hero/student, fortified by trust, may enter into a saving *I-Thou relationship:*

> On the heroic journey, the heroic novitiate is not alone.
> Soon after crossing the threshold, he/she meets with a wise
> old man or wise old woman. These wise ones successfully
> completed their own archetypal quests many years ago
> when they were young. They now often possess powerful
> amulets and know how to make potions. Frequently, they
> speak in riddles. *Guiding the young travelers, the Wise
> Ones are the archetypal teachers*—like Obiwan Kanobie in
> *Star Wars* or Guinan in *Star Trek.* Their amulets and po-
> tions symbolize the fact that they are able to aid the seeker
> because they have had their own visions. (Mayes, 1999, pp.
> 7-8)

This psychospiritual process fructifies in the student in the form of trust,

trust in the world, because this human being exists—that is the most inward achievement of the relation in education. Because [the teacher] exists, meaninglessness, no matter how hard pressed you are by it, cannot be the real truth. Because this human being exists, in the darkness the light lies hidden, in fear salvation, and in the callousness of one's fellow-men the great Love. (Buber, 1985, p. 98)

Teaching is the revelation of hidden treasure. But the ultimate wealth is not so much the curricular content inside the treasure chest (as precious as that content is) as it is the treasure chest itself—the containing relationship between the teacher, the student, and the divine. For in this ontological dialogue—which begins with the call to teach and matures in the interaction between teacher and student—meaning occurs both *in* and *as* the shared moral universe of teacher and student. For teacher and student, the fruit of this dialogical union is experiential knowledge of the fact that "the world is not divine sport, it is divine destiny. There is divine meaning in the life of the world, of man, of human persons, of you and of me" (Buber, 1965, p. 82). Whatever the subject matter that serves as its scaffold, the edifice of education is ultimately built brick by living brick in prayerful acts of teaching as relationship. This is what distinguishes it from the empty "magic" of corporate agendas for reform:

> What distinguishes sacrifice and prayer from all magic? Magic desires to obtain its effects without entering into relationship and practices its tricks in the void. But sacrifice and prayer are set "before the Face," in the consummation of the holy primary word that means mutual action: they speak the *Thou,* and then they hear. (Buber, 1965, 127)

Yogananda discovered from Sri Yukteswar that "magical" teaching is only about ego and gold, which the master illustrated in the story of Afzal the *fakir*. "Guruji," Yogananda asked his Master, "if Afzal could easily secure such things as gold dishes,

> why did he covet the property of others?" "The *fakir* was not highly developed spiritually," Sri Yukteswar explained. "[He] could summon the atoms of any object from etheric energy by an act of powerful will. But such astrally produced objects are evanescent; they cannot long be retained.... Afzal was not a man of God-realization," Master

went on. "Miracles of a permanent and beneficial nature are performed by true saints because they have attuned themselves to the omnipotent Creator." (1946, pp. 212-213)

The ethical teacher nurtures the "permanent and beneficial" miracles that come from truly humane acts of teaching in the spirit. In magical education, the student is the object of the corporate captain's passion for gold. In prayerful education, the student is liberated in authentic encounter with other students, the teacher, and the sacred. The magical pedagogy of corporate education robs the student of her identity, her "face." The prayerful pedagogy of relationship brings the student's "face" into ever clearer focus by bringing it into relationship with "the Face" of the transcendent.

The spiritual literature on teaching offers abundant examples of education as self-discovery through relatedness. Jack Kornfield, a Buddhist monk and Western psychotherapist, said of his beloved Cambodian forest master, Achaan Chah, "He kept directing us [young monks] back to an understanding of our own inner experience, to discover how we were entangled and how we, too, could learn to be free" (1993, p. 239). The miracle of soulful teaching is just this: Through the mirror of the subject matter, the teacher helps students see into their own hearts and thus find freedom from the psychological, social, and spiritual forces that have heretofore enslaved them. Is it any wonder that we look back on our favorite teachers with undying love? They have directed us from the starting-point of subject matter into the depths of our own hearts, where the eternal lives. A Tibetan master, the Dzogchen Ponlop Rinpoche, has declared,

> in Buddhist culture, the educational institutions of the past, all the way up to the institutions of the present, are basically there *to teach us to rediscover ourselves,* to rediscover this heart of enlightenment, rediscover the awareness which contains these two key qualities—knowledge and wisdom. This is, in essence, the entire foundation, path and goal of Buddhism. It is the entire educational journey of Buddhism. (1997, p. 57. Emphasis added)

Thus, according to Kornfield,

> in the end, the true purpose of a teacher is to guide us to discover our inherent freedom of heart. All spiritual teaching has this end, and the gift of all wise teachers is encour-

agement to find within ourselves our Buddha nature—free, independent, and joyful in the midst of all life. (1993, p. 243)

"Physician, heal thyself."

According to the physician and medical educator Ruth Naomi Remen (1999), these all-embracing pedagogical goals should be as present in medical education as in mystical education. Noting that "the medical profession is a culture of profound isolation" from one's colleagues, one's patients and oneself, Remen has attempted to deal with the alienation and fragmentation into which so many physicians fall by attending to this issue early in the medical school curriculum. The description of her course at the University of California, San Francisco, Medical School, entitled "The Healer's Art," states that "the purpose of the course is attending to human wholeness: One's own wholeness and the wholeness of others."

By the second year of medical school when they take this course, most students have already begun to don the clinical *persona* which the allopathic approach to medicine—along with growing corporate demand for speedy, impersonal, cost-effective treatment—forces on the doctor. Identical demands and pressures are increasingly coming to dominate the practice of psychotherapy as well, and with the same devastating effects on therapists (Corey & Corey, 1998) One thinks of de Castillejo's observation that "the fundamental nature of [physicians'] unhappiness [is that] the *archetype of a healer* which has sustained and nourished them throughout the centuries has fallen from their shoulders leaving them as little cogs in the great machine of modern medical practice" (1973, p. 22). In Buber's terms, the corporate demands for efficiency and economy above all else are robbing both physician and patient of their status as "Thous" and turning them into "its". In these terms, teacher alienation and burnout can be seen as a result of teachers having lost touch with the "archetype of the educator."

Remen's course attempts to bring students back to themselves as spiritually called physicians by simply bringing them back to *themselves:*

> I begin that first evening by offering the students silence as a substitute for fear and isolation. Now, this itself is a very rare thing in a medical school classroom—having permission to be silent together. Yet silence is the way we connect, both to each other and to ourselves.... After fifteen

minutes of silence, I ask the students a single question: "Is there a part of you that you are afraid you may forget in this process of becoming a doctor?"... I ask them first to reflect on this question within the privacy of their own consciousness. Then I ask them to find a symbol or an image for the part of themselves that is vulnerable to becoming lost, and to name its quality or qualities. I ask them how old this part is, how precious it is to them. I ask them to consider what this part of themselves has added to their lives and what would it mean for a person who is ill to meet with this part.... Each small group session ends with a healing exercise. This too involves sitting together in silence. The physician rings a bell, and then the student to his or her left says their name aloud. In silence, the group attends to the humanity of that student. They listen. They remember the part of their humanity that that particular student is struggling to preserve. And in perfect silence, they send strength; they believe in the student; they value their humanity; and they may even pray for it. They offer their silent support for each student's struggle to be whole. (pp. 39-42)

Of Caterpillars and Ecstasy

I will conclude this chapter by returning to the account of Jeanne Houston's early instructional encounters with Teilhard de Chardin. I believe that they illuminate, with that moral lightning that Chardin seems to have brought to all of his teaching encounters, the process of discovery of self and the sacred through an educative relationship that is grounded in but also transcends subject-matter.

In a captivating passage, Houston recalls the time when Chardin— ever the observant paleontologist—was on his knees in rapt admiration before a caterpillar that was crawling on the ground. After rhapsodizing on the beauty of the caterpillar and the miracle of its eventual metamorphosis into a butterfly, he asks his young teenage student if *she* can imagine escaping the physical and social limitations of being a teenager by emerging as an adult "butterfly":

> His comic-tragic face nodded helpfully until I could answer. "I...don't really know anymore, Mr. Thayer." "Yes, you do know. It is inside of you, like the butterfly is inside of the caterpillar." He then used a word that I heard for the first time, a word that became essential to my later work. "What is the entelechy of Jeanne? A great word, a Greek

word, *entelechy*. It means the dynamic purpose that is coded in you.... So what is the butterfly, the *entelechy* of Jeanne? You know, you really do." "Well...I think that..." I looked up at the clouds, and it seemed that...a fractal of my future emerged in the cumulus nimbus floating overhead. "I think that I will travel all over the world and...and...help people find their en-tel-echy." Mr. Thayer seemed pleased. "Ah, Jeanne, look back at the clouds! God's calligraphy in the sky! All that transforming, moving, changing, dissolving, becoming. Jeanne, become a cloud and become all the forms that ever were." (1996, pp. 142-143)

Teaching in the spirit means helping the student decipher herself in the calligraphy of the curriculum. When that happens, the evolving relationship between teacher and student is guided by their *entelechy* as children of heaven on a heroic journey—one filled with trials and even torment, but one which—having tested and enlarged their souls—will surely bring both of them back, transfigured, to their transcendent home.

Topics for Discussion

The author calls for teachers to cultivate *I-Thou* relationships with their students as a means of both resisting oppressive political agendas and exploring subject-matter. Is this a possibility in the postmodern American public school classroom with its diversity, demands, and multiple constraints such as large-class size, state-imposed standards, and legal guidelines? Even if the teacher were inclined to interact with her students in this way, would attempting to cultivate *I-Thou* relationships lead to the teacher challenging certain legal and institutional boundaries to such an extent that it might ultimately lead to burnout and/or dismissal? Is there perhaps a middle ground between potentially overtaxing *I-Thou* relationships with her students and potentially unethical *I-it* relationships with them? If so, how might the teacher create and protect such a relational zone in her classroom?

Can you imagine a classroom situation in which an *I-Thou* relationship might actually be counterproductive for both the teacher and her students?

Topics for Discussion (continued)

Can you recall a time as either a student or teacher when a synchronistic event (or some other type of extraordinary event) occurred during a class session?

In explaining the idea of synchronicity, the author referred to Carl Jung's reporting of synchronistic occurrences during therapy. What are the similarities between the classroom and the consulting room that might allow exceptional events in the classroom? What are some of the differences between the two venues that might make such events less likely in the classroom than in the consulting room?

What differences do you think it might make in a physician's life if he had taken Dr. Remen's course? How might it affect his practice as a physician? How might it affect his relationships with other physicians? With his patients? With his own research agenda? Furthermore, do you think that such forms of individual introspection and group processing might be useful in colleges of education with prospective teachers? If so, why do you think so, and what kinds of activities and exercises might the students engage in? If not, why do you think such things would be inappropriate or unproductive in a teacher education program?

Topics for Research

Survey and critically analyze some of the major statements over the last two decades on teaching as relationship and care. You might want to begin with Nel Noddings's (1992) work *Teaching as Care: An Alternative Approach to Education* as well as her (1995) article entitled "Care and Moral Education." Look as well at Gilligan's (1982) *In a Different Voice: Psychological Theory and Women's Development*. Do these ideas offer you any insights into your own teaching or into ways of teaching that you might want to cultivate? Why or why not?

Read Buber's (1965) book *I and Thou* as well as his (1985) essay "On Teaching" in the volume entitled *Between Man and Man*. Analyze these works in terms of their potential applicability (or inapplicability) to your own pedagogical philosophy and practice. Moreover, do you

Topics for Research (continued)

agree with Buber that the only teaching that is truly powerful is teaching that speaks what he calls the "primal word" of *I-and-Thou*?

Read and report on Ira Progoff's (1973) work *Jung, Synchronicity, and Human Destiny* in order to get a better sense of the idea of synchronicity as well as why it might or might not apply to your classroom practice.

Examine the life of a spiritual figure whom you particularly admire. In focusing upon his or her teaching moments, do you find that they are accompanied by extraordinary events? If so, do you see any pattern between: 1) the type of teaching and the *likelihood* of such an event taking place and/or 2) the type of teaching and the *type* of event taking place?

Six

Death and Resurrection in the Classroom

The Teacher as an Archetype of Spirit

I have examined elsewhere various spiritually oriented images of teachers that emerge when teachers reflect on their sense of calling (Mayes, 2002a). I found that they tend to fall into four categories: (1) The teacher as philosopher (what I have called "discursive spirituality"), (2) the teacher as a federal prophet of democracy ("civic spirituality"), (3) the teacher as counselor/mother/nurturer ("therapeutic spirituality"), and (4) the teacher as pastor, priest or Zen master ("ontological spirituality"). Spiritually centered teaching often combines these four "aspects of the teacher as an archetype of spirit" (Mayes, 2002a).

As necessary and healing as much of the literature that revolves around the third archetype of teaching-as-care has been, it frequently runs the risk of moving excessively in the direction of maternal nurturance, thus centering almost exclusively on only one of the four major spiritual archetypes of the teacher. The result is a therapeutic pedagogy that is so overly nurturing that the student (like any mother-bound child) does not learn to overcome those intellectual and ethical obstacles that are the dialectical precondition of psychological and moral growth (Riegel, 1979). In archetypal terms, the relationships that form between teacher and student become dominated by the archetype of the Great Mother, which, like all archetypes, has both a bright side and a shadow. As I have written elsewhere,

the Great Mother as Nurturer is the archetype that embodies the human need for and experience of all that is fecund,
nurturing, receptive and wholesome in the cosmos. [This
archetype promises a] return to the oceanic bliss of that un-
differentiated absorption in the universe that predated [the
individual's] emergence into the difficulties and alienation
of the newly formed and increasingly isolated ego. Having
fallen into the trauma of individual existence, [we] crave to
reenter the cosmic womb. The Great Mother calls [us] back
into her. This archetypal energy is probably more common
[in the psychodynamics of] female teachers than male
teachers; however, it is not unusual for male teachers also
to become conduits for the energy of the Great Mother.....
It can invest their classroom practice with compassion and
their psyches with a sense of purpose in helping, and on
rare occasions even healing, their students in emotional and
spiritual struggles.... [However,] even the life-giving, life-
sustaining archetype of the nurturing Great Mother [can, in
its excessive manifestations, cast] a shadow, and the
shadow that it casts is the archetype of the Devouring Great
Mother. This mother will not let her children go because,
possessed and inflated by her role as matriarch, she fears
emotional and spiritual death if they leave her. Like a snake
(indeed, in primitive and ancient art, she is often portrayed
wearing a wreath of snakes), the devouring mother recoils
and then strikes out in a fearing, fearful rage at the prospect
of a vacant house and empty womb. For her, the alternative
to caring for her children is not to set them free but...[to
entrap them in the web of her immoderate "care"]. (Mayes,
2001a, p. 703)

As in parenting, the most effective teaching style is authoritative, combining judgment (the archetypally paternal) and care (the archetypally
maternal) (Brophy, 1994). A pedagogy that relies excessively on care
easily degenerates into sentimentalism and indulgence.

The literature on spiritual teaching shows the masters achieving
balance in their teaching. For example, sitting on the hill outside of his
beloved city and weeping because of its iniquity, Jesus lamented in maternal strains, "O Jerusalem, Jerusalem, which killest the prophets, and
stonest them that are sent to thee; how often would I have gathered thy
children together, as a hen doth gather her brood under her wings, and
ye would not!" (Luke 13: 34) Yet very shortly thereafter, Jesus told his
apostles that he must suffer and die. Peter loudly protested that such a

thing could never happen to the Messiah! Jesus, now embodying the archetypally paternal, sharply rebuked Peter's lack of realism with the reprimand, "Get thee behind me, Satan: thou art an offence to me: for thou savorest not the things that be of God, but those that be of men" (Matthew 16: 23).

"You had to experience shipwreck."

Too often, the nurturing pedagogies do not allow sufficient opportunities for students to fail because of the presumed psychological harm that it will do to them. Certainly, repeated failure, or failure that is punished without tactful, constructive suggestions for improvement, breaks a student's spirit. A scripture from my religious tradition says that the teacher should teach "by kindness and pure knowledge, which shall greatly enlarge the soul, without hypocrisy, and without guile." Nevertheless, even though we must usually teach by "gentleness and meekness, and by love unfeigned," there are times when there is the necessity of "reproving betimes with sharpness...." This corrective sternness must be immediately followed, however, with evidence of abiding love for and faith in the student, "showing forth afterwards an increase of love toward him whom thou hast reproved.... That he may know that thy faithfulness is stronger than the cords of death" (*Doctrine and Covenants of the Church of Jesus Christ of Latter-day Saints* 121: 141-143). We must acknowledge and build upon the student's failures in positive and caring ways. However, eliminating the possibility of failure renders success meaningless. It also severely hampers the student's progress since psychological growth is dialectical (Riegel, 1979). Without tension, there is no need to grow—and, arguably, no *way* to grow.

In my faith, we believe that each human being consciously chose in a now forgotten pre-existence to become embodied in this present "telestial world" precisely because it is such a difficult place to be. It is this that makes it the most suitable realm of existence to maximize growth in each person's evolution toward becoming divine beings. Hence, the Latter-day Saint view of Eve is not as the gullible, culpable mother of all our woes, as in the standard Judeo-Christian tradition. Rather, we revere and love her as "our glorious Mother Eve," the first great "telestial" teacher, who, in partaking of the forbidden fruit, evidenced a spiritual genius and moral courage that seems to have evaded Adam in his somewhat simple, literalistic obedience. For, Eve in her greatness intuited the grand principle of eternal growth—namely that "it must needs be that the devil should tempt the children of men, or they could not be agents unto themselves; for if they never should have bitter they could not know the sweet..." (*Doctrine and Covenants of the Church of Jesus Christ of Latter-day Saints* 29:39). Our first, great Mother-Teacher understood the need for both failure as well as success in the eternal maturation of the spirit. Following her example, spiritual teaching evidences this mixture of the bitter with the sweet. As we will presently see, there are many instances in which the spiritual teacher allows the student to fail in order to learn necessary lessons that are not available in any other way.

Of course, the teacher must intervene between the student and a dangerous situation if the potential peril is too great. Don Juan thus tells Castaneda that the young apprentice's battle the previous night with a variety of supernatural spirits who were manifesting themselves as wind and fog were as real as the very ground on which they are now sitting in broad daylight. In particular, Don Juan points out how he saved Castaneda from walking on a bridge that had materialized from another dimension and which beckoned Castaneda to what could have easily been his doom. Ever the materialist, Castaneda attempts to dismiss Don Juan's observations by blithely concluding that the whole series of events the previous night was simply an illusion. Don Juan reproves this superficial view of reality by remarking that

> "there are worlds upon worlds, right here in front of us. And they are nothing to laugh at. Last night if I hadn't grabbed your arm, you would have walked on that bridge whether you wanted to or not. And earlier I had to protect you from the wind that was seeking you out." "What would have happened if you had not protected me?" "Since you don't have enough power, the wind would have made you lose your way and perhaps even killed you by pushing you into a ravine. But the fog was the real thing last night.... If I had not protected you, you would have had to walk on that bridge regardless of anything.... I stopped you because I know you don't have the means to use power, and without power the bridge would have collapsed." (1972, pp. 165-166)

The spiritual teacher intervenes when the student is wandering off into truly dangerous intellectual, emotional or moral territory. On one hand, the teacher steers the student clear of the tenuous bridge of simplistic analysis—an ephemeral structure that simply cannot bear the weight of reality and that will result in the student's collapse and humiliation. On the other hand, the teacher helps the student negotiate complexity so that its dangerous winds do not toss him down the stony slopes of confusion.

Not only does the spiritual teacher not let a student get caught in failure; he does not let him get caught in success. As teachers we are deeply invested in our students' success. When they succeed, we feel we've done a good job, and we justifiably want to praise them (and perhaps ourselves!). Such positive reinforcement is good; but when proffered excessively, praise loses its value as a precious commodity. It also creates a sense of false security and psychological inflation that can lead the student into catastrophe farther down the road when the overly solicitous teacher is no longer there to protect him.

After a particularly exhilarating attainment of cosmic consciousness, Yogananda was quite amazed at the experience—and also, perhaps, at his own power in having achieved it. "My guru was standing motionless before me," he reported,

> I started to prostrate myself at his holy feet in gratitude for his having bestowed on me the experience in cosmic consciousness that I had long passionately sought. He held me upright and said quietly: "You must not get overdrunk with ecstasy. Much work yet remains for you in the world. Come, let us sweep the balcony floor; then we shall walk by the Ganges. I fetched a broom.... (1946, p. 168)

Herrigel's archery master is particularly astringent in this regard, quite in keeping with the Zen cultivation of divine indifference. He discourages even the slightest degree of self-satisfaction in a successful performance.

> "That was a right shot," said the Master decisively, "and so it must begin. But enough for today, otherwise you will take special pains with the next shot and spoil the good beginning." Occasionally several of these right shots came off in close succession and hit the target, besides of course the many more that failed. But if even the least flicker of satisfaction showed in my face, the Master turned on me with unwonted fierceness. "What are you thinking of?" he would cry. "You know already that you should not grieve over bad shots; learn now not to rejoice over the good ones. You must free yourself from the buffetings of pleasure and

> pain, and learn to rise above them in easy equanimity, to re-
> joice as though not you but another had shot well. This too
> you must practice unceasingly—you cannot conceive how
> important it is." (1971, pp. 68-69)

In the *Tao Te Ching,* Laotse wrote that the wise spiritual guide sometimes seems "unkind..., treat[ing] the people like sacrificial straw dogs" (Yutang, 1948, p. 63). This is necessary not only because of the dialectical nature of learning but also because the student must be stripped of his ego-bred illusions. Failure-proof learning environments leave the student unprepared to cope with the error and danger that he is now even *more* likely to encounter because he has been coddled. True learning both requires and fosters humility; but humility can only grow out of the experience of failure. As Isaiah declared, "Every valley shall be exalted; and every mountain and hill shall be made low [be-fore] the glory of the Lord [is] revealed" (Isaiah 40:4). When the mountains of pride and self-absorption are leveled, then the valleys of humility rise to the even plane of divine knowledge.

We have already seen this principle at work in Herrigel's experi-ence as a student of Zen archery. As is often true in spiritual pedagogy, the master not only does not particularly reward initial success by the student but may even take quite a dim view of it, for it merely confirms the student's self-centered world-views. Early in his training, Herrigel, quite puzzled, reported that "the saying of the Master went round in the school that whoever makes good progress in the beginning has all the more difficulty later on" (1971, p. 28).

The spiritual teacher often uses paradoxes to catch the student in contradictions which cannot be resolved by his old models of reality. I attempt to do this in my own history of education classes. I not only undermine my students' initially celebratory views of American educa-tion but offer them complex, and sometimes mutually exclusive, mod-els, each of which solves certain problems of empirical interpretation but also generates other problems. Thus, the student cannot find a sim-ple, correct model—one that comfortably corresponds to his previous views. He comes to learn the truth of Socrates' dictum that it is in the awareness of one's intellectual poverty that true knowledge begins.

Similarly, Herrigel had to experience a personal dead-end before the pedagogy of paradox opened the vista of spiritual liberation. "I un-derstand well enough," Herrigel said to the Master one afternoon as they sat drinking tea, that the hand mustn't be opened with a jerk if the shot is not to be spoiled. But however I set about it, it always goes wrong. If I clench my hand as tightly as possible, I can't stop it shaking when I open my fingers. If, on the other hand, I try to keep it relaxed, the bowstring is torn from my grasp before the full stretch is reached—unexpectedly, it is true, but still too early. I am caught between these two kinds of failure and see no way of escape." (1971, pp. 32-33)

The Master immediately locates the source of the seemingly impossible contradiction. It is the ego—that great enemy of all spirituality.

"The right art," cried the Master, "is purposeless, aimless! The more obstinately you try to learn how to shoot the arrow for the sake of hitting the goal, the less you will succeed in the one and the further the other will recede. What stands in your way is that you have a much too willful will. You think that what you do not do yourself does not happen." (p. 34)

If both teacher and student learn to let go of their small, self-serving notions of how things are or should be and seek the humility of being guided by the Spirit, it will direct them both. We *must* let our students fail so that they may grow intellectually and spiritually. Herrigel's friend and fellow student, Mr. Komichaya, said to him, "You had to suffer shipwreck through your own efforts before you were ready to seize the lifebelt [the master] threw you" (1971, p. 26).

For these reasons, the teacher, although relating to his students in loving ways, is never simply a "friend," which is too often the image that emerges from the literature on teaching as care. Why is the truly caring teacher not the student's "friend"? In the first place, the teacher must know more than the student. If the teacher cannot make this claim, then by what right does he presume to stand in front of the classroom and guide the discourse? To be sure, the spiritual teacher must approach the student and subject matter with unfeigned humility and existential awe, for in encountering the student the teacher is facing a being who has come to the classroom already possessing a rich personal history and boundless ontological possibilities. But true humility does not require (indeed, it does not permit) a trumped-up illusion of equality between the teacher and student regarding the subject under study. If the teacher cannot legitimately assume the role of a true guide, then he is a false guide. "And if the blind lead the blind," said Jesus, "shall they not both fall into the ditch?" (Luke 6:39).

Buber himself, whose *I-Thou* philosophy is frequently cited as the justification for the teacher-as-friend, was quite emphatic that a true *I-Thou* relationship between teacher and student, although allowing great room for friendliness, precluded friendship as such, for

> however much depends upon [the teacher's] awakening the
> *I-Thou* relationship in the pupil... and however much de-
> pends upon the pupil, too, meeting and affirming [the
> teacher] as the particular person he is—the special educa-
> tive relationship could not persist if the pupil for his part
> practiced "inclusion," that is, if he lived the teacher's part
> in the common situation. Whether the *I-Thou* relationship
> now comes to an end or assumes the quite different form of
> friendship, it is plain that the specifically educative rela-
> tionship as such is denied full mutuality. (1965, p. 132)

The World—and How to Stop It

There are many techniques that the spiritual teacher uses to "de-familiarize the world" so that students will begin to question their as-sumptions and consider other possibilities in the new dialogical uni-verse in which they find themselves with their teacher—a figure who does not offer easy nurturance but demands courageous confrontation. These archetypally paternal pedagogical strategies bear a strong resem-blance to Don Juan's idea of "stopping the world."

> In order to arrive at "seeing" one had to first "stop the
> world." "Stopping the world" was indeed an appropriate
> rendition of certain states of awareness in which the reality
> of everyday life is altered because the flow of interpreta-
> tion, which ordinarily runs uninterrupted, has been stopped
> by a set of circumstances alien to that flow. (1972, p. 14)

One of the best ways to stop the student's world is to make him aware of his own death—the death of his ego in the dissolution of its cherished illusions. Thankfully, this process does not require physical death in the classroom (although during a particularly boring lecture it might feel like it to the student!). However, it does point to physical death in that physical death is the ultimate dissolution. Hence, a basic tenet of many religions, from Catholicism to Tibetan Buddhism, is *me-*

mento mori—ponder death—not as a macabre obsession but as a way of overcoming illusions and living with eyes wide open.

This idea also pervades Existential psychotherapy (May & Yalom, 1995), whose therapeutic techniques bear a striking resemblance to much spiritual teaching (Hanh, 1987). Existential therapy sees neurosis as an ultimately symbolic attempt to avoid facing the reality of death. By this view, neurotic fears and syndromes are the displaced expressions and timid evasions of the terrifying fact of mortality. In Existential philosophy, a life lived in denial of one's own mortality is ultimately neurotic and inauthentic; it is a life lived in "bad faith," always in illusory flight from the fundamental fact that our birth simply sets us on a trajectory toward our death. If nature and God have ordained it to be so, then how could any valid spiritual vision ever arise out of living in the denial of death? To face the fact of one's death unties the bonds of this neurosis, engenders a realistic vision of one's powers and limitations, and thus enables one to discover his "life-project." *It is only in fully embracing the fact that one will die that one can begin to live.* Viewed in this light, not allowing the student and his old world-views to die is essentially neurotic—a doomed attempt to deny the mortal limitations that we have been sent here to experience and learn from. A teacher who is preoccupied with protecting his students from failure because of the presumed emotional harm it might do to them is often symbolically refusing to face his own death (Mayes, 2002b).

In spiritual instruction, therefore, it is precisely in the student's experience of intellectual death (or "shipwreck," as the Zen master said) that he finds new intellectual life. The instructional cycle of the spiritual classroom is a paschal mystery: It leads from the Cross, on which the student's old conceptions must be nailed, to the Risen Lord of his renewed consciousness in the Spirit. The effects of such balanced instruction on the student are quick, dramatic and durable. Said Yogananda,

> I am immeasurably grateful for the humbling blows [Sri Yukteswar] dealt my vanity. I sometimes feel that, metaphorically, he was discovering and uprooting every diseased tooth in my jaw. The hard core of egotism is difficult to dislodge except rudely. With its departure, the Divine finds at last an unobstructed channel. In vain it seeks to percolate through flinty hearts of selfishness. (1946, p. 141)

Sometimes, the blows that the spiritual masters deliver to shatter the student's old worldviews are so strong as to seem merciless—although, in fact, they stem from a higher form of compassion, "a severe mercy" (Vanauken, 1979). One of my favorite examples of this occurs when Don Juan asks Castaneda if he feels that they are equals. Castaneda rather patronizingly assures Don Juan that they are, although Castaneda secretly feels that he, a graduate student at UCLA, is superior to this poor, uneducated Yaqui who roams the desert and lives in a shack. Still, Castaneda disingenuously insists that he and Don Juan are equals.

> "No," [Don Juan] said calmly, "we are not." "Why, certainly we are," I protested. "No," he said in a soft voice. "We are not equals. I am a hunter and a warrior and you are a pimp." My mouth fell open. I could not believe that Don Juan had actually said that. I dropped my notebook and stared at him dumbfoundedly and then, of course, I became furious. He looked at me with calm and collected eyes. I avoided his gaze. And then he began to talk. He enunciated his words clearly. They poured out smoothly and deadly. He said that I was pimping for someone else. That I was not fighting my own battles but the battles of some unknown people. That I did not want to learn about plants or about hunting or about anything else. And that his world of precise acts and feelings and decisions was infinitely more effective than the blundering idiocy I called "my life." After he finished talking I was numb. He had spoken without belligerence or conceit but with such power, and yet with such calmness, that I was not even angry anymore. (p. 81)

I imagine that there are very few of us as teachers who have attained the imperial heights of spiritual clarity that Sri Yukteswar and Don Juan did. Hence, few of us have the same kind of right (and even fewer the inclination) to "dislodge" the student's misconceptions "rudely." If we tried, we would probably wind up doing so quite ineffectively—with "belligerence or conceit." Nevertheless, the example of these two masters does make clear to all of us who are spiritually motivated that there are times when we must openly and plainly recognize a student's error for what it is—not "nurture" the student even more deeply in his misconceptions for fear that we will damage his fragile "self-esteem," which, founded on a falsehood, is ultimately doomed to collapse anyway.

Joseph Smith, Jr., the first president and prophet of my church, exemplified the art of lovingly but firmly accomplishing this pedagogical and spiritual goal.

> On one occasion...Joshua Holman, a former Methodist exhorter, was out with some other men cutting firewood for the Prophet [Joseph Smith] when they were all invited to lunch at Joseph's home. When the Prophet called on Joshua to ask a blessing on the food, he set about a lengthy and loud prayer that incorporated inappropriate expressions. The Prophet did not interrupt him, but when the man was through, he said simply, "Brother Joshua, don't ever let me hear you ask another such blessing." Then he explained the inconsistencies. (Madsen, 1989, p. 26)

This episode provides a simple but effective model of the pedagogical point in question: The teacher invites the student to express himself in a manner that will edify the class; he then attentively allows the student to attempt to do so, not interrupting even if he sees that the student is in error; he then matter-of-factly calls attention to the error in the student's thinking and expression; finally, he kindly but firmly explains the source of the problem and how to avoid it in the future.

The preceding examples demonstrate one way of interacting with a psychically inflated student who is certain that he knows more than he really does, more than the teacher even, and who is determined to demonstrate this publicly in class at every available opportunity. This student will grow neither personally nor intellectually if the teacher does not cordially but firmly "uproot" the ideologically "diseased tooth" that is lodged in the stubborn jaw of his arrogance. A warm and yielding approach to such a student actually does him an intellectual and emotional disservice and is not really nurturing but unethical and irresponsible. In many instances the most spiritually productive way of "uprooting" a student's arrogance is amicably but unequivocally to expose the incompleteness, contradictions, and dangers of his clumsy notions and half-baked ideas.

The Uses of Humor

One of the most effective tools for getting a student to reconsider a position is humor. This was a pedagogical technique at which Joseph Smith also excelled. Indeed, his disarmingly boyish sense of humor was one of his most endearing qualities. The role of the gentle trickster was one that Joseph loved to play, and it is indeed a role that many of the masters whom we are studying fill at various times in order to help their students deconstruct and then reconstruct their worlds in the service of spiritual growth.

A robust man of considerable athletic prowess and what he himself characterized as "a native, cheery temperament," Joseph Smith loved to run, jump and wrestle with anyone who would join him in friendly competition. But for Joseph, rustic sports were more than just physical activities. They were also a way of philosophically disarming an adversary and attempting to win over his *heart*—always the foremost concern of a spiritual master. Joseph, a young man with little formal education (but immense learning), had, along with his brothers and sisters, grown up helping his mother and father tend to their humble farm. Indeed, he was merely a 14-year-old farm boy when he received his first heavenly visitations. Thus, he learned quite early in life that a prophet may well need to free people from the pious illusion that good people always look and dress in one particular way, and that prophets always come straight from central casting with a great white beard, hoary locks, a flowing robe, and a loud frightening voice. Truman Madsen, one of Joseph Smith's foremost biographers, tells of the time when a man who had developed a falsetto voice (and an even falser form of spirituality) came to visit the young prophet.

> In our generation we are not familiar with this phenomenon, but in preaching without public address systems in [the early 19th century] some [preachers] would pitch their voices high and shout so loudly that it could be heard a mile away. Sometimes they prayed that way. One man with exactly that tone came and said, with a kind of supercilious reverence, "Is it possible that I now flash my optics upon a Prophet?" "Yes," the Prophet replied, "I don't know but you do; would you like to wrestle with me?" The man was shocked.

A prophet can be a farm boy who, after a hard day's work, likes some rough and tumble play and a few good jokes. Divine messages are famous for coming to us in a way we had never expected. Joseph, like many other spiritual masters, used humor to help people cast off their limited—and irreverently *limiting*—ideas about how God may choose to express Himself.

On another occasion, with serious intent but humorous overtones, the Prophet dressed up in rough clothes, got on a horse, and rode down to meet a group of converts who had just arrived from England. He stopped one of them who was heading for town.

"Are you a Mormon?" the Prophet asked.

"Yes, sir," said Edwin Rushton.

"What do you know about old Joe Smith?"

"I know that Joseph Smith is a prophet of God."

"I suppose you are looking for an old man with a long, gray beard. What would you think if I told you I was Joseph Smith?"

"If you are Joseph Smith, I know you are a prophet of God."

"I am Joseph Smith," the Prophet said, this time in gentle tones. "I came to meet those people, dressed as I am in rough clothes and speaking in this manner, to see if their faith is strong enough to stand the things they must meet. If not, they should turn back right now." (Madsen, 1989, p. 26)

Just as the man or woman of God often comes to us in the clothes of a trickster, so does the spiritual teacher.

A Brief History of the Trickster

Paul Radin's (1956) classic study, *The Trickster: A Study in American Indian Mythology,* is still considered the most important work in the analysis of the trickster in Native American cultural anthropology. As Radin shows in his exploration of the Winnebago Trickster Cycle, the most famous of all the Indian trickster narratives, the trickster is a paradox—a blend of buffoonery and high seriousness. Trickster's duality stems from his historical development from an animalistic prankster to a culture hero.

In his earliest appearances in Native American societies as merely a sensual joker, the primal trickster is really no more than a personification of libido. Yet, even though he first appears historically as someone who "possesses no values, moral or social, [and] is at the mercy of his passions and appetites," the amazing thing is that by the time of his later historical incarnation as a culture hero, trickster has become a pillar of society, and it is "through his actions [that] all values come into being" (Radin, 1956, p. ix). How can such a questionable character as the primal trickster evolve into a demigod trickster who is key in forming and maintaining a culture, as Radin assures us is often the case? And what does all of this have to do with spiritual teaching? I believe the answer lies in Jung's dualistic vision of the psyche as expressed in his idea of "the shadow" (Jung, 1956).

The shadow is all of those aspects of ourselves that are constantly bubbling up from the unconscious. We may attempt to repress or deny these parts of ourselves, but that does not make them disappear. Indeed, Jung insisted that it is only by courageously encountering one's shadow that a person learns to harness its energy constructively. This is no easy task, for "to confront the shadow...means to take a mercilessly critical attitude towards one's nature" (Jacobi, 1968, p. 113). Yet it must be done because denying one's shadow ultimately just energizes it with the power of resistance. Furthermore, if we fail to face our shadow and do not integrate its potentially productive energy into consciousness, we will sooner or later commit the psychological and ethical error of projecting that shadow onto others—even to the point of demonizing them. We are all made up of light and dark. Spiritual balance and compassion are attained only on condition of reconciling this duality (Jung 1963). "[O]nly if we keep this insight persistently in mind can our confrontation with other pairs of psychic opposites be successful. For, this is the beginning of the objective attitude toward our own personality without which no progress can be made along the path of wholeness" (Jacobi, 1986, pp. 113-114).

Now, it is precisely such a creative reconciliation of opposites that the trickster represents in his later historical incarnations as a culture-hero. Still a passionate character, he has nevertheless managed to learn important socio-ethical lessons and, what is more, now embodies them for his culture. Thus, at the end of the Winnebago Cycle, trickster emerges triumphant in the form of what Radin (1956) calls the "hero trickster" and Belmonte dubs (1990) the "sacred clown."

The Teacher as a Sacred Clown

A spiritual teacher, the sacred clown *deconstructs to reconstruct.* Thus it is that his "performance clarifies the epistemological possibilities of his people's cosmology. He factors out the fundamental signs of social health and disease" (Belmonte, 1990, p. 52). What is the sacred clown, then, but a teacher? "As myth and symbol [the sacred clown] came into being to serve...educational goals: to bring about moral and religious transformation in his students" (Lundquist, 1991, p. 7). To bring about this "religious transformation" in students, the teacher's first job is to make the world strange to them so that they will ultimately have no choice but to question their political, epistemological and spiritual assumptions. We see an excellent example of the teacher doing just this in Don Juan's pedagogical strategy of "stopping the world." As Castaneda observed, "'Stopping the world' was indeed an appropriate rendition of certain states of awareness in which the reality of everyday life is altered because the flow of interpretation, which ordinarily runs uninterrupted, has been stopped by a set of circumstances alien to that flow" (1972, p.14).

Humor can stop the student's world because it is an epistemic hurricane that uproots his illusions, breaks him down, and tosses him onto unfamiliar existential ground. At this point, he is teachable. "I laugh a great deal," Don Juan once said to his apprentice, "because I like to laugh. But everything I say is deadly serious, even if you don't understand it. Why should the world be only as you think it is? Who gave you the authority to say so?" (p. 84) Sometimes this "deadly serious" humor is at the expense of the teacher himself—or at least *seems* to be, although the ultimate target of the comic *exemplum* is really the student. Like all clowns, the teacher as a sacred clown is really just a mirror of the spectator's own foibles. For in the final analysis, the spectator at a circus does not so much laugh at the funny, painted clown slouching and stumbling under the big top as he laughs at a spotlighted caricature of himself—laughs, that is, at his own cosmic fragility and constant screw-ups thrown into comic relief; laughs at his own precariousness in this rollicking, dangerous universe; laughs in embarrassment and pleasure that there is much more to things than has met his undeveloped third eye of spiritual vision.

If the teacher is both theatrically and conceptually adroit enough, and if the student can see—in the comic mirror of the teacher's humor—the shakiness of his own unexamined opinions, then that student may learn how to discard old world-views and form new ones. The laughter of the clown is a death knell to the ego, and this death is the precondition of spiritual rebirth. Through humor, students learn to die to old perspectives and be reborn into new ones. The crowning paradox of the teacher as a sacred clown, then, is that he is both a mortician and a midwife. His humor is a matter of ideological life and death. But this grave flipside of laughter should not surprise us. Every clown knows that comedy is serious business.

A Personal Example

I teach graduate and undergraduate courses in curriculum theory and multiculturalism at a conservative religious university where every term at least a few of my undergraduate students come to my required seminars with an *a priori* dislike of the subject matter, believing multi-cultural studies to be a pseudo-discipline based on dangerous, morally relativistic assumptions. Moreover, many come to my class with fairly fixed notions about what a curriculum should be. My first task, then, is to upset those students' monolithic educational ideas in order to plant in them the seeds of a more complex vision, one that I believe will ulti-mately serve them better, and one that will also allow them to serve *their* students better, in the culturally diverse environment of the post-modern American public school classroom. But how to accomplish this?

I don the costume of the sacred clown—this time in the form of the clown's cousin, the shapeshifter (Jamal, 1996). Throughout the term I "embody" many different views on multiculturalism, beginning with their own generally conservative ones. In what I hope is a noble dis-simulation, I begin by letting my conservative undergraduate students assume that I share their perspective on all multiculturalism as muddle-headed, politically dangerous, and ethically destructive. I then com-mence to wrestle—publicly, desperately, unsuccessfully—with the glaring pedagogical, ethical, and even religious inconsistencies of that hyper-conservative position. My students are aghast to see me and "my" position ingloriously collapse under the weight of internal con-tradictions. I sometimes even literally collapse in front of them, trip-ping over a chair, distorting my mouth, bulging my eyes, and howling in melodramatic misery. (My grandmother was a vaudeville comedi-enne in the Yiddish theater in the early 1900's, and I often sense she is happy to know that the tradition continues in my teaching.)

By now, all of my students, from the most conservative to the most liberal, see what I am up to, and I "'fess up" to my "virtuous counter-feit." But I do not stop shapeshifting. In fact, it is at this precise point of ideological crisis and paradigmatic tension that I assume a radically dif-ferent shape by introducing them to certain Marxist ideas as well as Freire's (1970) notion of *conscientizacion*. I go on to spend the rest of the term playing the role of Proteus (the Greek shapeshifter) for my students, putting on a whole wardrobe of ideological guises. Assuming those theoretical "postures" for and with the class, I encourage my stu-dents to join me in exploring the difficult but liberating fact that virtually every perspective on education—from the most radical to the most conservative—reveals certain truths and creates certain difficulties. My students come to grasp the wisdom in Kenneth Burke's great pronouncement that "every way of seeing is also a way of not seeing" (Burke, 1982).

The wise words of the Native American shapeshifter and storyteller Johnny Moses beautifully capture the essence of a shapeshifting pedagogy that helps students see things from many new points of view.

> During a storytelling presentation with young people, the children themselves transform as they begin to participate, making the different animal sounds of the bear and the ant, the octopus lady and the crow. They tell me a story by their actions, by their body language, by their facial expressions, changing according to the animal I am telling a story about. *The children have a chance to experience something other than their own selves, or ego....* There is a shapeshifting interchange between the storyteller and the audience, audience and storyteller, even as the stories themselves are about shapeshifting. (As cited in Jamal, 1995, p. xv. Emphasis added.)

The purpose of all of these pedagogical techniques and approaches is not gratuitously to cause the student pain. Nothing could be farther from the spiritual nature of the teacher's mission. Such an exercise of power would be "unrighteous dominion" (*Doctrine and Covenants of the Church of Jesus Christ of Latter-day Saints* 121: 37). Rather, the purpose of this archetypally paternal pedagogy (which, as Mother Eve's example shows us, is as effective in the hands of a female teacher as in those of a male teacher) is to defamiliarize the student's worldview—and to challenge the unhealthy ego structures that tenuously buttress that worldview. That accomplished, the teacher and the student can then move on together to greater intellectual and spiritual heights.

Conclusion: The Paschal Classroom

Both Existential psychotherapy and spiritual teaching aim at forcing the patient or student to confront death by relinquishing—or at least revising—illusory conceptual and psychological commitments. The primary goal is to move the person along in the process of fully accepting responsibility for his life by facing his death. When this has happened, then the patient and student have achieved some measure of liberation: Having faced their fundamental fears, they no longer depend on others to define or negotiate their existences for them. This does not mean that they live solipsistically, disregarding others' points of views, or that they do not need others emotionally. However, they take ultimate responsibility for their relation to, interpretation of, and actions in the world. "The teacher's intention is to arouse the student's capacity to make a choice" (Harris, 1991, p. 67). The teacher helps the student see, think, feel, and act as an independent moral agent, who, precisely because he *is* healthily independent, will act most responsibly toward others.

This may be especially difficult to accomplish with students who simply want to put themselves in our hands. These are the students who *demand* to be nurtured with a constant flow of "right answers" from the teacher, like infants clamoring for mother's milk. They will not *tolerate* ambiguity. They want to be *given* solutions so that they can dutifully record them (as if they came directly from Mt. Sinai) on the stone tablets of their note pads, and then later reproduce them on the Almighty Test, the grade on which becomes the god of their scholastic idolatry. The spiritual teacher will not succumb to the invitation—indeed, seduction—by his students to become the classroom deity. Instead, he challenges each student to take responsibility for his own unique "eternal progression" into truth.

The spiritual teacher understands that, under the guise of revering the teacher, students who want only the "approved information" ultimately just want their world-view to be confirmed—perhaps a bit elaborated but certainly not fundamentally challenged by the teacher! They want to bind the teacher with the velvet bonds of bad faith. Such students pretend to be consulting the teacher but in fact are only trying to reaffirm their comfortable illusions by politely manipulating him. However, when the student puts himself into the hands of a spiritually oriented teacher, he often gets more than he bargained for. For to the extent that the teacher is in tune with the divine, the student has in a certain sense fallen into a sacred presence manifesting itself in and as this teacher, this subject, this class, and this time in history. The student has wandered onto holy ground, which is not always lush and verdant but can sometimes be stark and hard. After all, it was in the *desert* that the Word became flesh.

Some students may complain when they realize that they are not in a class of easy answers and multiple-choice tests but in a moral space where the teacher requires genuine engagement with both himself and the subject matter. However, the spiritually focused teacher will not deny or even minimize the pedagogical necessity for intellectual and moral conflict, and he will certainly not accept either fear or flattery (those twin forms of false worship) as a substitute for a truly educational experience. Instead, he stays on the scene to live through those conflicts, to negotiate them with his students. In this way, teacher and student together find the salvation that can come only through heartful, fearless engagement with the subject-matter, with each other, and therefore finally with the divine. The teacher who does not promote such understanding is not ultimately a spiritual teacher but instead a purveyor of the quick fixes of intellectual *legerdemain* and spiritual diminishment—a *fakir*. Woe to the teacher who does not encourage and enable this ontological freedom in the student but instead lets the student either fear or flatter him! Teaching then becomes idolatrous—the teacher setting up his charisma as a substitute for the presence of the sacred.

When the student has fully accepted responsibility for himself by renouncing pre-packaged, simplistic answers, then he becomes a vital moral and intellectual agent who can engage in mature dialogue with the teacher. Having known the shipwreck of his illusions on the rocks of the teacher's sometimes flinty instruction, having fled to the teacher for shelter and safety but not finding it, and having thus come to see his own aloneness and responsibility before the teacher, before others, before the world, and finally before God, the student is now authentically open to the genuine insights that the teacher can offer him. *Now,* the teaching moment is possible, without anxiety or idolatry.

I believe that this process of "repentance" is necessary for both the teacher and the student to move into a deeper encounter with the subject-matter and each other. "Re-pentance" in this sense means to "rethink" one's position about a subject in the light of eternal truth as it emerges in the educative relationship and casts new hues on subject-matter. In this sense, one is always "re-penting" in spiritual teaching and learning because one is always discovering that previously held positions (often rooted in the barren soil of egotism) must be pulled up and cast away in the transformation of the self. This is repentance. If the student will suffer this form of death (a death that the teacher also suffers in *his* ongoing relationship with the subject-matter), then, along with Castaneda, he sees that the collapse of the world and the resulting sense of "hallucination" is, paradoxically, "more real than anything [he] believed in" previously. Through challenge, failure, repentance and

Topics for Research (continued)

or so. You might want to begin your research with Donald Schön's (1987) work, *Educating the Reflective Practitioner.*

Review some of the author's work (see Mayes, 2004, 2002a, 2002b, 2001a, 1999, 1998 in the bibliography) that deals with the use of what he calls "spiritual reflectivity" to help public school teachers and administrators explore and deepen their sense of professional calling and purpose. Do you feel that such reflectivity might be appropriate and useful at a school where you are presently teaching/administering or one where you might do so in the future? If you do feel that it would be productive for staff to engage in this kind of reflectivity at that school, how would you promote and conduct such activities? What are some difficulties and dangers that might arise, and how would you deal with them if they did?

Conclusion

Curriculum, Instruction, and Transcendence

Education for Transcendence

Throughout this study, subject-matter has been seen as a medium through which the teacher and student discover each other and the divine. In this sense, the curriculum is both contingent and crucial. It is *contingent* because it is finally a means of achieving a greater goal: The grasping of the sacred. If curriculum is not in some sense involved with and pointed toward the teacher's and student's eternal evolution, then it ceases to be spiritual. Yet, the curriculum is also *crucial* because each curriculum—with its unique assumptions, issues, methods and objectives—forms a unique conceptual grammar that allows us to converse with each other and the divine in a particular way. For "what we term education, conscious and willed," said Buber,

> means *a selection by man of the effective world:* it means to give decisive effective power to a selection of the world which is concentrated and manifested in the educator. The relation in education is lifted out of the purposelessly streaming education by all things, and is marked off as purpose. (1985, p. 89)

This "selection of the effective world" is also the defining of a world. "I have come to see," Parker Palmer says,

> that knowledge contains its own morality, that it begins not in a neutrality but in a place of passion within the human soul. Depending on the nature of that passion, our knowledge will follow certain courses and head toward certain ends. From the point where it originates in the soul, knowledge assumes a certain trajectory and target.... (1983, p. 7)

Each curricular domain originates in a certain form of encounter with and interpretation of each other and nature. Through dialogical relationship, teacher and student participate in an ongoing process of refinement. If all goes well in this process, the result is that both are finally translated in terms of the specific vocabulary of that subject-matter into a closer communion with the mystery that encompasses our lives. In this way, curriculum and instruction are means of transcendence. They inhabit a "sacred space" (Klein, 2000, p. 5). These spaces are divine precincts, peopled by teachers whose calling is to help create these precincts, sustain them, and enjoy them. In such spaces, teachers sense the promise and see the reflection of those eternal realms from which we came and to which we shall someday return as transfigured beings.

None of this requires that curriculum and instruction must deal with explicitly religious themes although, of course, it may do so. Generally, however, it is through the interactive exploration of specific domains of knowledge that the teacher and student *as* teacher and student grasp a particular manifestation of the divine together. Explicit mention of religion is also prohibited in many cases because of wise legal standards that allow it in the classroom only if it is relevant to the subject being studied, presented in a neutral manner, and open to contestation by the student (Abington v. Schempp, 1963; Mayes & Ferrin, 2001b). What is more, a dogmatic presentation of religious doctrines will be off-putting to many students, will make others feel that they must also embrace those views (which belong, after all, to the person who is giving the grades!), and may create a smug sense of ideological superiority in those students who happen to share the teacher's beliefs. Most importantly, it will dam the spontaneous flow of dialogue and discovery that is necessary if students are genuinely to find the divine *in, for,* and *as* themselves. Public education as religious indoctrination stands at the opposite end of the spectrum from public education as commercial in-doctrination—but both equally impede the evolution of the student as a moral agent.

In short, to be spiritual, the curriculum does not have to deal with explicitly "spiritual" topics. However, it must be spiritually grounded in the teacher's heart—or else it will become the mere transmission of data and theories for the sake of some imposed political or economic goal. Such goals sometimes constitute a legitimate, if qualified, aim of education; however, they should never be its primary aim. That is edu-cation without moral connection to others or the transcendent. It is magical or idolatrous pedagogy. But the pedagogies that grow from the fecund soil of the love of others and the sacred are—despite the teacher's formal religious commitments or lack thereof—spiritual pedagogies. The teacher's practice does not need to be established on a particular religious creed to be spiritual, but it must be energized by some form of spiritual commitment. It is important to fully recognize and honor the fact that the teacher's spirituality may be highly indi-vidualistic (Mayes, Blackwell Mayes, & Sagmiller, in press); for, as the sociologist Anthony Giddens (1991) has noted, this is the direction that religious conviction in general has moved throughout the 20th century and will increasingly continue to do in the 21st century.

The fundamental criterion for spiritual pedagogy as I have defined it in this study is that it emerge from and grow toward the experience of the divine that grows out of love for others. "For when ye are in the service of your fellow beings, ye are only in the service of your God" (*Book of Mormon*, Mosiah 2:17). I believe that many, and possibly most, teachers hear their calling and find their professional sustenance in this or a related idea of service. If we are really serious about "teacher renewal," then we must put first things first and help teachers access and cultivate these noble impulses and visions by encouraging "spiritual reflectivity" in both prospective and practicing teachers (Mayes, 2001a).

Neither neo-liberal nor neo-conservative educational reform rec-ognizes the sacred dimension in education. For them, education is the aggressive accumulation of data and paradigms in the service of post-industrial capitalism. Along with the poet T.S. Eliot, we might well ask, "Where is the wisdom we have lost in knowledge?/Where is the knowl-edge we have lost in information?" (1971, p. 96) It is the spiritual vocation of teachers to find and promote such knowledge and wisdom—*temporal* knowledge in the service of *eternal* wisdom. It should not be the grim duty of the teacher to have to cram students with sterile data so that they can score well on tests that serve technocratic purposes.

The teacher's higher calling is not a vocation that our society generally understands, much less celebrates. True, it often pays lip-service to teachers as guardians of the democratic tradition, but that is the political rhetoric of the American view of education. The reality—one that has been growing over the last century and became all but triumphant in the insidious form of President Bush's *No Child Left Behind Act*—is that curriculum is becoming a form of *control*: Control of man and nature by technological imposition, control of the schools by corporate agendas, control of the teacher by competency-based criteria, and finally control of both teacher and student by high-stakes standardized testing (Jones, Jones, & Hargrove, 2003). Parker Palmer has said that the classroom should be a space where "obedience to truth is practiced" (1983, p. 69). But both the neo-liberal and neo-conservative "vision" of education for the 21st century is that the classroom is a space where obedience to corporate profitability should be practiced. The teacher *as prophet* is becoming the teacher *for profit*.

The spiritual teacher, therefore, must see her work not only as a spiritual exercise but also as an act of political resistance. This should not be surprising, for the most potent forms of political commitment are rooted in spirituality. Gandhi's life bore witness to this fact through the practice of *Satyagraha*. Martin Luther King, profoundly influenced by the ideal of *Satyagraha*, which he translated as "soul force," brought it to the American Civil Rights Movement. In Central America, the courageous life and death of the activist Catholic Archbishop Oscar Romero, assassinated by a right-wing hit-squad in 1980 while he was celebrating mass, also testified to the power of "soul force" as the basis of "justice-making" (Lepage, 1991, p. 73). For the teacher who has a sense of moral mission, it is her burden and blessing to be called to exercise soul force in how and what she teaches. Purpel and Shapiro (1995) are quite correct that the teacher needs to continue to grow both spiritually *and* politically throughout her career in order to have deep and lasting effects on her students, her institutions, and her culture.

The discovery and exercise of soul force in one's life as a teacher has probably never been easy. It requires enormous moral commitment, leading to a growth *with* one's students and *toward* the sacred. This growth must be its own reward, not the accolades of the world. As the person who, in my view, was the world's greatest spiritual teacher reminds us, the spiritual teacher's ultimate remuneration is in the currency of eternity, not in coins of the realm:

> Ye have not chosen me, but I have chosen you, and ordained you, that ye should go and bring forth good fruit.... If the world hates you, ye know that it hated me before it hated you. If ye were of the world, the world would love its own: but because ye are chosen out of the world, but because I have chosen you out of the world, therefore the world hateth you." (John 15: 16, 18-19)

Growing into this vocation is an ongoing existential commitment of the teacher's whole being. She cannot be a teacher with only a part of herself. Her teaching is an encompassing moral fact of her life. If it is not, then she may be a competent technician who can train (and may occasionally entertain) her students, but she cannot influence them in any eternally consequential ways. Indeed, when the spiritually called teacher is forced into this technocratic role, she often abandons the field, leaving our children with one less valiant soul to guide them.

As with any spiritual vocation, one can complete it only by virtue of the very grace that called one to teach in the first place. Just as the call initially came in the form of teaching a particular subject, so it must, by effort and grace, grow in the teacher's ever deepening encounter with that subject. Therefore, the spiritually called teacher can not approach her subject-matter as just a body of information to master and then impose on her students. Rather, she must see it as a medium (and for some teachers, one of the most important mediums) of her own intellectual, moral and spiritual growth in an eternal journey of discovery. In other words, the teacher develops an *I-Thou* relationship with her subject. "Teaching, when seen as an activity of religious imagination, is the incarnation of subject matter in ways that lead to the revelation of subject matter" (Harris, 1991, p. xv). Parker Palmer has said,

> not only do I invest my own personhood in truth and the quest for truth, but truth invests itself personally in me and the quest for me. "Truth is personal" means not only that the knower's person becomes part of the equation, but that the personhood of the known enters the relation as well.

The known seeks to know me even as I seek to know it;
such is the logic of love. (1983, p. 58)

When this happens, the curriculum is spiritualized and, in a smaller
but still significant way, becomes a type of scripture, "quick and powerful, and sharper than any two-edged sword, piercing even to the di-
viding asunder of soul and spirit, and of the joints and marrow,... a dis-
cerner of the thoughts and intents of the heart" (Hebrews 4:12). As
truth seeks us just as much as we seek it, so may the curriculum seek
the teacher just as much as she seeks it. As she lives *with* and *in* her
curriculum in ever deepening ways, she personally embodies it in how
she sees and lives her own life. This is the calling of the teacher-
prophet, who teaches and embodies her subject as a witness not only to
the survival but the final *triumph* of the sacred in the technocratic
wastelands of the postmodern world. The teacher-prophet has *faith*, as
the Protestant Existential theologian Paul Tillich has defined that word.

> The content of faith in Providence is this: when death rains
> from heaven as it does now, when cruelty wields power
> over nations and individuals as it does now, when hunger
> and persecution drive millions from place to place, as they
> do now, and when prisons and slums all over the world
> throughout history degrade the humanity of the bodies and
> souls of men as they do now—we can boast in that time,
> and just in that time, that even all of this cannot separate us
> from the love of God. In this sense, and in this sense alone,
> all things work together for good, for the *ultimate* good, the
> eternal love, and the Kingdom of God. Faith in divine
> Providence is the faith that nothing can prevent us from ful-
> filling the ultimate meaning of our existence. Providence
> does not mean a divine planning by which everything is
> predetermined as an efficient machine. Rather, Providence
> means that there is a creative and saving possibility implied
> in every situation, which cannot be destroyed by any event.
> Providence means the daemonic and destructive forces
> within ourselves and our world can never have an unbreak-
> able grasp upon us, and that the bond which connects us
> with the fulfilling love can never be disrupted. (1976, p.
> 107)

In the communion of teacher, student and curriculum, the divine breaks through and manifests itself *in* and *as* an educational relationship. With *this* particular teacher, with *these* very students, in *this* ordinary classroom, studying *this* specific subject, the temporal touches the eternal, our personal and collective histories are reconciled and redeemed, and the goal of spiritual teaching is finally attained: The unity of the teacher, student, and subject in the service and presence of the divine.

References

Abington Township, Pennsylvania, et al. v. Schempp et al., 374 US 203 (1963).

Adler, M. (1982). *The paideia proposal: An educational manifesto.* New York: MacMillan.

Aichhorn, A. (1990). The transference. In A. Esman (Ed), *Essential papers on transference* (pp. 94-109). New York: New York University Press.

Ajaya, S. (1985). *Psychotherapy east and west: A unifying paradigm.* Honesdale, Pennsylvania: Himalayan International Institute.

Apple, M. (1990). *Ideology and curriculum.* London: Routledge.

Arlow, J. (1995). Psychoanalysis. In R. Corsini, R., and D. Wedding (Eds.), *Current psychotherapies: Basics and beyond* (pp. 15-50). Itasca, Illinois: F.E. Peacock.

Axelrod, R., and Cooper, C. (1991). *The St. Martin's guide to writing.* New York: St. Martin's Press.

Belmonte, T. (1990). The trickster and the sacred clown: Revealing the logic of the unspeakable. In K. Barnaby and P. D'Acierno (Eds.). *C.G. Jung and the humanities: Toward a hermeneutics of culture* (pp. 45-66). Princeton, N.J.: Princeton University Press.

Black Elk. (1932). *Black Elk speaks: Being the life story of a holy man of the Oglala Sioux. As told through John G. Niehardt (Flaming Rainbow).* New York: William Morrow and Company.

Bolt, R. (1990). *A man for all seasons.* New York: Vintage Press.

Bonhoffer, D. (1963). *The cost of discipleship.* New York: Collier Books.

Brennan, J. (1988). *Hands of light.* New York: Mariner Press.

Brophy, J. (1994). *Motivating students to learn.* Boston: McGraw-Hill.

Brown, G., Phillips M., and Shapiro, S. (1976) *Getting it all together: Confluent education.* Bloomington, Indiana: Phi Delta Kappa Educational Foundation.

Buber, M. (1985). *Between man and man.* New York: Vintage.

Buber, M. (1965). *I and thou*. New York: Vintage.

Bullough, R. (2001). *Uncertain lives: Children of hope, teachers of promise*. New York: Teachers College, Columbia University.

Bullough, R.V., Jr. (1989). *First-year teacher: A case study*. New York: Teachers College Press.

Bullough, R.V., Jr., Mayes, C. and Patterson, R.S. (2002a). Wanted: A prophetic pedagogy: A response to our critics. *Curriculum Inquiry, 32(3)*, 311-330.

Bullough, R.V., Jr., Patterson, R.S., and Mayes, C. (2002). Teaching as prophecy. *Curriculum Inquiry, 32(3)*, 341-348.

Burke, K. (1989). *On symbols and society*. J. Gusfield (Ed), Chicago: University of Chicago Press.

Callahan, R. (1962). *Education and the cult of efficiency. A study of the social forces that have shaped the administration of the public schools*. Chicago: University of Chicago Press.

Campbell, J. (1949). *The hero with a thousand faces*. Princeton: Princeton University Press.

Castaneda, C. (1972). *Journey to Ixtlan: The lessons of Don Juan*. New York: Touchstone Books.

Cohen, M. (1988). In B. Wolstein (Ed), *Essential papers on countertransference* (pp. 64-83). New York: New York University Press.

Corey, J., Corey, M., and Callanan, P. (1998). *Issues and ethics in the helping professions*. Boston: Brooks/Cole Publishing Co.

Cremin, L. (1988). *American education: The metropolitan experience: 1876-1980*. New York: Harper and Row.

Dalai Lama, His Holiness, the. (1997). Education and the human heart. *Holistic Education Review*, 10(3), pp. 5-7.

de Castillejo, I. (1973). *Knowing woman: A feminine psychology*. New York: Harper and Row.

de Chardin, T. (1975). *The phenomenon of man*. New York: Perennial Library.

Dewey, J. (1916). *Democracy and education*. New York: Macmillan.

Edinger, E. (1973). *Ego and archetype: Individuation and the religious function of the psyche*. Baltimore: Penguin Press.

Eliot, T. (1971). *T.S. Eliot: The complete poems and plays: 1909-1950*. New York: Harcourt, Brace and World, Inc.

Epstein, L., and Feiner, A. (1988). Countertransference: The therapist's contribution to treatment. In B. Wolstein (Ed), *Essential papers on countertransference* (pp. 282-303). New York: New York University Press.

Feinstein, D., and Krippner, S. (1988). *Personal mythology: Using rituals, dreams, and imagination to discover your inner story*. Los Angeles: Jeremy P. Tarcher, Inc.

Ferrer, J. (2002). *Revisioning transpersonal theory: A participatory vision of human spirituality*. Albany, New York: State University of New York Press.

Fordham, M. (1996). Countertransference. In Shamdasani, S. (Ed), *Analyst-patient interaction: Collected papers on technique.* London: Routledge.

Freire, P. (1970). *The pedagogy of the oppressed.* New York: Seabury Press.

Freud, S. (1990a). The dynamics of transference. In A. Esman (Ed), *Essential papers on transference* (pp. 28-36). New York: New York University Press.

Freud, S. (1990b). Observations on transference-love. In A. Esman (Ed), *Essential papers on transference* (pp. 28-48). New York: New York University Press.

Giddens, A. (1991). *Modernity and self-identity: Self and society in the late modern age.* Stanford: Stanford University Press.

Giddens, A. (1990). *The consequences of modernity.* Stanford: Stanford University Press.

Gilligan, C. (1982). *In a different voice: Psychological theory and women's development.* Cambridge, Mass.: Harvard University Press.

Graves, R. (1959). *The white goddess: A historical grammar of poetic myth.* New York: Farrar, Straus, and Giroux.

Greenson, R. (1990). The working alliance and the transference neurosis. In A. Esman (Ed), *Essential papers on transference* (pp. 150-171). New York: New York University Press.

Hanh, T. (1987). *The miracle of mindfulness: A manual on meditation.* Boston: Beacon Press.

Happold, F. (1963). *Mysticism: A study and an anthology.* New York: Penguin.

Harris, M. (1991). *Teaching and religious imagination: An essay in the theology of teaching.* San Francisco: Harper Collins.

Hayward, J. (1999). Unlearning to see the sacred. In S. Glazer (Ed), *The heart of learning: Spirituality in education* (pp. 61-76). New York: Jeremy P. Tarcher.

Hendricks, G. and J. Fadiman, eds. (1976). *Transpersonal Education: A Curriculum for Feeling and Being.* Englewood Cliffs, New Jersey: Prentice-Hall, Inc.

Herrigel, E. (1971). *Zen and the art of archery.* New York: Vintage Book.

Hofstadter, R. (1963). *Anti-intellectualism in American life.* New York: Vintage Books.

Houston, J. (1996). *A mythic life: Learning to live our greater story.* San Francisco: Harper Collins.

Huberman, M., Gronauer, M., Marti, J. (1989). *The lives of teachers.* J. Neufeld (Trans.). New York: Teachers College Press.

Huxley, A. (1945). *The perennial philosophy.* New York : Harper.

Jacobi, J. (1968). *The psychology of C.G. Jung: An introduction with illustrations.* New Haven, Connecticut: Yale University Press.

Jacoby, M. (1984). *The analytic encounter: Transference and human relationship.* Toronto, Canada: Inner City Books.

Jamal, M. (1996). *Deer dancer: The shapeshifter archetype in story and in trance.* New York: Arkana.

James, W. (1958). *The varieties of religious experience: A study in human nature.* New York: New American Library.

Jones, J. (1980). *Soldiers of light and love: Northern teachers and Georgia Blacks: 1865-1873.* Chapel Hill: University of North Carolina Press.

Jones, M., Jones, B., and Hargrove, T. (2003). *The unintended consequences of high-stakes testing.* Lanham, Maryland: Rowman and Littlefield Publishers.

Jung, C. G. (1992). *The psychology of the transference.* R. Hull (Trans.). Princeton, New Jersey: Princeton University Press.

Jung, C. G. (1973). *Aion: Researches into the phenomenology of the self.* R. Hull (Trans.). Princeton, New Jersey: Princeton University Press.

Jung, C. G. (1963). *Mysterium coniunctionis: An inquiry into the separation and synthesis of psychic opposites in alchemy.* R. Hull (Trans.). Princeton, New Jersey: Princeton University Press.

Jung, C. G. (1959). *The archetypes and the collective unconscious.* R. Hull (Trans.). Princeton, New Jersey: Princeton University Press.

Jung, C. G. (1956). *Symbols of transformation: An analysis of the prelude to a case of schizophrenia.* R. Hull (Trans.). New Jersey: Princeton University Press.

Jung, C. G. (1976). *Psychological types.* R. Hull (Trans.). New Jersey: Princeton University Press.

Jung, E., and von Franz, M. (1960/1986). *The grail legend.* Boston: Sigo Press.

Kirsch, J. (1995). Transference. In M. Stein. (Ed), *Jungian analysis* (pp.170-209). Chicago, Illinois: Open Court Publishing Co.

Klein, S. (2000). Curriculum as sacred space. *Encounter: Education for Meaning and Social Justice,* 13(1), pp. 5-10.

Kliebard, H. (1986). *The struggle for the American curriculum: 1893-1958.* New York: Routledge.

Knox, J. (1998). Transference and countertransference. In I. Alister and C. Hauke (Eds.), *Contemporary Jungian analysis:: Post-Jungian perspectives from the society of analytic psychology* (pp. 73-84). London: Routledge.

Kornfield, J. (1997). *Living Buddhist masters.* Santa Cruz, California: Unity Press.

Kornfield, J. (1993). *A path with heart: A guide through the perils and promises of spiritual life.* New York: Bantam.

Lasch, C. (1995). *The revolt of the elites and the betrayal of democracy.* New York: Norton.

LePage, A. (1991). Creation spirituality and the reinventing of education. In R. Miller (Ed), *New directions in education: Selections from Holistic Education Review,* 267-275. Brandon, Vermont: Holistic Education Press.

Lundquist, S. (1991). *The trickster: A transformation archetype.* San Francisco, California: Mellen Research University Press.

Machtiger, H. (1995). Reflections on the transference/ countertransference process with borderline patients. In N. Schwartz-Salant and M. Stein (Eds.), *Transference/countertransference* (pp. 119-146). Wilmette, Illinois: Chiron Publications.

Madsen, T. (1989). *Joseph Smith the prophet.* Bookcraft: Salt Lake City, Utah.

Marcuse, H. (1962). *Eros and civilization: A philosophical inquiry into Freud.* New York: Vintage.

Marshak, M. (1998). The intersubjective nature of analysis. In I. Alister and C. Hauke (Eds.), *Contemporary Jungian analysis: Post-Jungian perspectives from the society of analytic psychology* (pp. 57-72). London: Routledge.

Marx, K., and Engels, F. (1978). *The Marx-Engels reader.* R. Tucker (Ed). New York: W.W. Norton and Co.

Maslow, A. (1968). *Toward a psychology of being* (2nd edition). Princeton, New Jersey: D. Van Nostrand.

Mattingly, P. (1975). *The classless profession: American schoolmen in the nineteenth century.* New York: New York University Press.

May, R., and Yalom, I. (1995). Existential psychotherapy. In R. Corsini and D. Wedding, (Eds.), *Current psychotherapies* (pp. 262-292). Itasca, Illinois: F.E. Peacock.

Mayes, C. (2004a). *Seven landscapes: A new approach to the holistic curriculum.* Lanham, Maryland: University Press of America.

Mayes, C., Blackwell Mayes, P., and Sagmiller, K. (2004b, in press). Spiritual commitments of prospective teachers at a state university compared with those of students at a religious university. *Religion and Education.*

Mayes, C. (2002a). The teacher as a spiritual archetype. *Journal of Curriculum Studies,* 34(6), pp. 699-718.

Mayes, C. (2002b). Personal and archetypal aspects of transference and counter-transference in the classroom. *Encounter: Education for Meaning and Social Justice,* 15(2), 34-49.

Mayes, C. (2001a). A transpersonal developmental model for teacher reflectivity. *Journal of Curriculum Studies,* 33(4), pp. 248-264.

Mayes, C., and Ferrin, S.E. (2001b). Spiritually committed public school teachers: Their beliefs and practices concerning religious expression in the classroom. *Religion and Education,* 28(1), 75-94.

Mayes, C. (1999) Reflecting on the archetypes of teaching. *Teaching Education,* 10(2), pp. 3-16.

Mayes, C. (1998). The use of contemplative practices in teacher education. *Encounter: Education for Meaning and Social Justice,* 11(3), pp. 17-31.

McLynn, F. (1997). *Carl Jung: A biography.* London: Black Swan.

Merton, T. (1967). *Mystics and Zen masters.* New York: Dell Publishing Co.

Miller, J. (2000). *Education and the soul: Toward a spiritual curriculum.*

Needle, N. (1999). The six paramitas: Outline for a Buddhist education. *Encounter: Education for Meaning and Social Justice,* 12(1), pp. 9-21.

Neumann, E. (1954). *The origins and history of consciousness* (vol. 1). New York: Harper and Brothers.

Noddings, N. (1995). Care and moral education. In W. Kohli (Ed), *Critical conversations in the philosophy of education* (pp. 137-148).

Noddings, N. (1992). *The challenge to care in schools : An alternative approach to education.* New York: Teachers College Press.

Orr, D. (1988). Transference and countertransference: A historical survey. In B. Wolstein (Ed), *Essential papers on counter-transference* (pp. 91-110). New York: New York University Press.

Otto, R. (1958). *The idea of the holy.* New York: Oxford University Press.

Oxford English Dictionary. (1990). New York: Oxford University Press.

Palmer, P. (1998). *The courage to teach: Exploring the inner landscape of a teacher's life.* San Francisco: Jossey Bass.

Palmer, P. (1983). *To know as we are known: A spirituality of education.* San Francisco: Harper Collins.

Parkerson, D., and Parkerson, J. (2001). *Transitions in American education: A social history of teaching.* London: Routledge.

Pinar, W., W. Reynolds, P. Slattery, and P. Taubman, Eds. (1995). *Understanding Curriculum: An Introduction to the Study of Historical and Contemporary Curriculum Discourses.* New York: Peter Lang.

Progoff, I. (1973). *Jung, synchronicity, and human destiny.* New York: Julian Press.

Purpel, D., and Shapiro, S. (1995). *Beyond liberation and excellence: Reconstructing the public discourse on education.* Westport, Connecticut: Bergin and Garvey.

Radin, P. (1956). *The trickster: A study in American Indian mythology, with commentaries by Karl Kerenyi and C.G. Jung.*

Ravitch, D. (2000). *Left back: A century of failed school reforms.* New York: Simon and Schuster.

Remen, R. (1999). Educating for mission, meaning and compassion. In S. Glazer (Ed), *The heart of learning: Spirituality in education* (pp. 33-49). New York: Jeremy P. Tarcher.

Reinsmith, W. (1992). *Archetypal forms in teaching: A continuum.* New York: Greenwood Press.

Riegel, K. (1979). *Foundations of dialectical psychology.* New York: Academic Press.

Samuels, A. (1997). *Jung and the post-Jungians.* London: Routledge.

Schön, D. (1987). *Educating the reflective practitioner.* San Francisco, California: Jossey-Bass Publishers.

Schwartz-Salant, N. (1995). Archetypal factors underlying sexual acting-out in the transference/countertransference process. In N. Schwartz-Salant and

M. Stein (Eds.), *Transference/countertransference* (pp. 1-30). Wilmette, Illinois: Chiron Publications.

Scotton, B., A. Chinen and J. Battista, Eds. (1996). *Textbook of transpersonal psychiatry and psychology.* New York: Basic Books.

Simmer-Brown, J. (1999). Commitment and openness: A contemplative approach to pluralism. In S. Glazer (Ed), *The heart of learning: Spirituality in education* (pp. 97-112). New York: Jeremy P. Tarcher.

Sklar, K. (1973). *Catherine Beecher: A study in American domesticity.* New Haven: Yale University Press.

Snauwert, D. (1992). The educational theory of the *Bhagavad Gita. Encounter: Education for Meaning and Social Justice,* 5(1), pp. 51-58.

Spiegelman, J. (1996). *Psychotherapy as a mutual process.* Tempe, Arizona: New Falcon Publications.

Spring, J. (2000). *American education* (9th ed). New York: McGraw Hill.

Spring, J. (1976). *Educating the worker-citizen.* New York: McKay Press.

Stein, M. (1995). Power, shamanism and maieutics in countertransference. In N. Schwartz-Salant and M. Stein (Eds.), *Transference/counter- transference* (pp. 67-88). Wilmette, Illinois: Chiron Publications.

Steinberg, W. (1990). *Circle of care: Clinical issues in psychotherapy.* Toronto, Canada: Inner City Books.

Stone, L. (1988). The transference-countertransference complex. In B. Wolstein (Ed), *Essential papers on counter-transference* (pp. 270-281). New York: New York University Press.

Tillich, P. (1976). *The Shaking of the Foundations.* New York: Scribners.

Tower, L. (1988). The meanings and uses of countertransference. In B. Wolstein (Ed), *Essential papers on counter-transference* (pp. 131-157). New York: New York University Press.

Tremmel, R. 1993. Zen and the art of reflective practice in teacher education. *Harvard Educational Journal,* 63(4): 434-458.

Tyack, D. (1989). The future of the past: What do we need to know about the history of teaching? In D. Warren (Ed), *American teachers: Histories of a profession at work* (pp. 408-421). New York: Macmillan Publishing Co.

Tyack, D. (1974). *The one best system: A history of American urban education.* Cambridge, Mass.: Harvard University Press.

Van Manen, M. (1990). Moral approaches to reflective practice. In R. Clift, W. Houston and M. Pugach (Eds.), *Encouraging reflective practice in education: An analysis of issues and programs* (pp. 20-35). New York: Teachers College Press.

Van Manen, M. (1982). Phenomenological pedagogy. *Curriculum Inquiry,* 12(3), pp. 283-299.

Vanaucken, S. (1979). *A severe mercy.* New York: Bantam Books.

Watras, J. (1996). *The foundations of educational curriculum and diversity: 1565 to the present.* Boston: Allyn and Bacon.

Wexler, P. (1996). Holy sparks: Social theory, education and religion. New York: St. Martin's Press.

Whitmore, D. (1986). *Psychosynthesis in education: A guide to the joy of learning.* Rochester, Vermont: Destiny Books.

Wiedemann, F. (1995). Mother, father, teacher, sister: Transference/countertransference with women in the first stage of animus development. In N. Schwartz-Salant and M. Stein (Eds.), *Transference/countertransference* (pp. 175-190). Wilmette, Illinois: Chiron Publications.

Wilber, K. (1983). *A sociable god: A brief introduction to a transcendental sociology.* New York: McGraw-Hill Book Company.

Wolstein, B. (1988). The pluralism of perspectives on countertransference. In B. Wolstein (Ed), *Essential papers on counter-transference* (pp. 339-354). New York: New York University Press.

Woodman, M. (1995). Transference and countertransference in analysis dealing with eating disorders. In N. Schwartz-Salant and M. Stein (Eds.), *Transference/countertransference* (pp. 53-66). Wilmette, Illinois: Chiron Publications.

Wordsworth, W. (1967). "The world is too much with us." In D. Perkins (Ed), *English Romantic Writers* (p. 209). New York: Harcourt, Brace, and World, Inc.

Yogananda, Paramahansa. (1946). *Autobiography of a yogi.* Los Angeles, California: Self Realization Fellowship.

Young, B. (1956). *Journal of discourses: By Brigham Young, his two counselors, the twelve apostles, and others; reported by G.D. Watt, and humbly dedicated to the Latter-day Saints in all the world.* Los Angeles, California: Gartner Printing and Litho.

Yutang, L. (1948). *The wisdom of Laotse.* New York: The Modern Library.

Index

About the Author

Clifford Mayes is an associate professor of curriculum history and theory in the Department of Educational Leadership and Foundations at Brigham Young University in Provo, Utah. He received the Ph.D. in the Cultural Foundations of Education at the University of Utah and also holds a doctorate in psychology from Southern California University for Professional Studies. His research revolves around the psychospiritual dimensions of the teacher's sense of calling and has appeared in *The Journal of Curriculum Studies, Curriculum Inquiry, The International Journal of Leadership in Education, Religion and Education, Teaching and Teacher Education, The Teacher Education Quarterly, The Teacher Educator, Teaching Education, Encounter,* and *Psychological Perspectives: A Semi-annual Journal of Jungian Thought.* He is also the author of a text in curriculum theory, *Seven Curricular Landscapes: An Approach to the Holistic Curriculum,* published in 2003 by University Press of America. He is presently working on a book entitled *Archetype and Education: Jungian and Neo-Jungian Theory for Teachers.* From 1981 until 1991, Dr. Mayes taught British and American Studies at the University of Panama in David, Panama, and Nagoya Gakuin University in Nagoya, Japan. He received a *Teacher of the Year Award* in 1998 from the Brigham Young University Student Alumni Association and is listed in *Who's Who in American Education.* He and his wife, Pam, are members of the Church of Jesus Christ of Latter-day Saints. They have three children— Lizzy, Josh and Dana.